Heart of Wisdom

Also by Geshe Kelsang Gyatso

Meaningful to Behold
Clear Light of Bliss
Buddhism: A Beginner's Guide
Universal Compassion
The Meditation Handbook
Joyful Path of Good Fortune
Guide to Dakini Land
The Bodhisattva Vow
Heart Jewel
Great Treasury of Merit
Introduction to Buddhism
Understanding the Mind
Tantric Grounds and Paths
Ocean of Nectar
Essence of Vajrayana
Living Meaningfully, Dying Joyfully
Eight Steps to Happiness
Transform Your Life

Profits received from the sale of
this book will be donated to the
NKT-International Temples Project
A Buddhist Charity Building for World Peace
UK email: kadampa@dircon.co.uk
US email: kadampacenter@aol.com

GESHE KELSANG GYATSO

Heart of Wisdom

A COMMENTARY TO
THE *HEART SUTRA*

THARPA PUBLICATIONS
Ulverston, England
Glen Spey, New York

First published in 1986
Second edition 1989
Third edition revised and reset 1996
Fourth edition with new line illustrations and reset 2001

Tharpa Publications
Conishead Priory
Ulverston
Cumbria LA12 9QQ, England

Cover photo of the Kadampa Temple Buddha Shakyamuni
by Kelsang Lhachog.
Cover design by Tharpa Publications.
Cover photo of Geshe Kelsang Gyatso by Kathia Rabelo.
Line illustrations by Gen Kelsang Wangchen.

Library of Congress Control Number: 2001092514

British Library Cataloguing in Publication Data
A catalogue record for this book is
available from the British Library.

ISBN 0948006 80 3 – papercase
ISBN 0948006 77 3 – paperback

Set by Tharpa Publications.
Printed on acid-free 250-year longlife paper and bound
by Butler and Tanner, Frome, Somerset, England.

Contents

Illustrations

Acknowledgements

This book, *Heart of Wisdom*, is based on an oral commentary to the *Essence of Wisdom Sutra* (the *Heart Sutra*), which was given by the author, Venerable Geshe Kelsang Gyatso, at Manjushri Mahayana Buddhist Centre in England.

We thank the author from the depths of our heart for his great kindness in preparing this complete and authoritative explanation of the *Heart Sutra* in English. With this inspired commentary as the key, the reader can unlock the full extent of the profound and vast aspects of the meaning of this essential Buddhist Sutra. Without the author's deep insight into the subject, and his compassionate determination to share this insight, this book could not have been produced.

Our appreciation also goes to all the dedicated, senior students of the author who assisted him with the translation and editing, and who prepared the final manuscript for publication.

Roy Tyson,
Administrative Director,
Manjushri Mahayana
Buddhist Centre,
September 1996.

Buddha Shakyamuni

Introduction

I feel very fortunate to have the opportunity to give this commentary to the *Essence of Wisdom Sutra*, or *Heart Sutra*. Similarly, those who have the opportunity to study the meaning of this Sutra, which is the essence of Buddha's teachings, are also extremely fortunate. Because of the profound nature of this Sutra it is possible that some people will find certain parts of this commentary difficult to understand. I will try to explain these teachings as clearly as possible, to the limit of my ability, but because this Sutra deals with emptiness – the ultimate nature of reality – we must be prepared to encounter some difficulties. You should try not to become discouraged, and please do not become frustrated and angry! Through patient study and contemplation it is possible to gain a complete understanding of the entire Sutra. As our familiarity with these teachings grows, so too will our understanding.

All teachings of Buddha are either Sutra or Tantra teachings and thus there is not a single scripture of Buddha that

is not one of these two. Sutra teachings are divided into two
types: Hinayana Sutras and Mahayana Sutras. Of these two,
the *Essence of Wisdom Sutra* belongs to the category of
Mahayana Sutras. The Mahayana Sutras themselves comprise many different types of teaching, but the most precious and supreme are the *Perfection of Wisdom Sutras* (Skt.
Prajnaparamitasutra). *for this school*

There are several *Perfection of Wisdom Sutras* of varying
lengths. The most extensive of these is the *Perfection of Wisdom Sutra in One Hundred Thousand Lines*, which in the
Tibetan translation occupies twelve volumes. There is also a
medium length Sutra of twenty-five thousand lines in three
volumes, and a short, single-volume Sutra of eight thousand lines. In addition there is an even shorter Sutra in eight
chapters of verse known as the *Condensed Perfection of Wisdom Sutra*. The *Perfection of Wisdom Sutras* explain all the
stages of the paths of wisdom and method, the paths which
together are the means to attain full enlightenment, or
Buddhahood. In particular, in these Sutras Buddha sets
forth his ultimate view of the nature of reality, and thus
among Sutras the *Perfection of Wisdom Sutras* are held to be
supreme.

The *Essence of Wisdom Sutra* is much shorter than the
other *Perfection of Wisdom Sutras* but it contains explicitly or
implicitly the entire meaning of the longer Sutras. It is
because it contains the very essence of the perfection of wisdom teachings that it is known as the *Essence of Wisdom
Sutra*. Through studying, contemplating, and meditating on
this Sutra we can gain a perfect understanding of the nature
of reality; we can overcome hindrances and difficulties in

our daily life; and finally we can overcome the obstacles preventing our full awakening, thereby attaining the perfect state of Buddhahood. We are indeed fortunate to have met these essential teachings of Buddha.

Shariputra

The Title and Homage

The Tibetan text of the *Essence of Wisdom Sutra* starts with the title of the Sutra and the homage paid by those who translated the Sutra from Sanskrit. Following these is the main body of the Sutra. This commentary contains an explanation of these three sections of the text, plus a short conclusion, and is given under four main headings:

1 The meaning of the title
2 The homage of the translators
3 An explanation of the main body of the Sutra
4 Conclusion

In addition, an explanation is given in the final chapter of how the Sutra can be used as part of a practice to overcome obstacles affecting ourself and others.

THE MEANING OF THE TITLE

Essence of the perfection of wisdom, the Blessed Mother

This is a translation of the title of the Sutra into English. In the Tibetan text the title is given first in Sanskrit and then in Tibetan, as follows:

Sanskrit: *Bhagavatiprajnaparamitahrdaya*

Tibetan: *Chom dän dä ma she rab kyi pa röl tu jin pai nying po*   "Honorable attributing"

There are two main purposes in giving the title in Sanskrit at the beginning of the Tibetan text. The first is to make clear that this is an authentic teaching of Buddha Shakyamuni himself, translated from the original Sanskrit, and not, as some might suppose, a later composition by Tibetans. The second purpose is to remind us of the kindness of the translators. There were many translators of this Sutra, one of the most famous being Rinchen Sangpo. Without their efforts in making this translation, the Tibetan people would not have had the opportunity to study and practise the profound teachings contained within this text. Furthermore, it is through their kindness that Western people can also come into contact with these precious teachings some two thousand five hundred years after the passing away of Buddha.

The meaning of the title of the Sutra can be explained by considering each of its terms. 'The perfection of wisdom' is a translation of the Tibetan 'she rab kyi pa röl tu jin pa' (Skt.

prajnaparamita), which more literally means 'wisdom gone to the other side'. The actual perfection of wisdom is a wisdom realizing emptiness that is conjoined with the mind of enlightenment, or bodhichitta. There are two types of actual perfection of wisdom: the causal perfection of wisdom and the resultant perfection of wisdom. The causal perfection of wisdom is the wisdom realizing emptiness possessed by Bodhisattvas. It is called the 'causal perfection of wisdom' because it acts as the direct cause of attaining the resultant perfection of wisdom. The resultant perfection of wisdom is the Wisdom Truth Body of a Buddha, Buddha's omniscient wisdom. In addition to the causal and resultant perfection of wisdom there is also the textual perfection of wisdom. This is the scriptures that reveal the causal and resultant perfection of wisdom. The textual perfection of wisdom is not the actual perfection of wisdom because it is not a mind realizing emptiness. It is merely given this name because it reveals the actual perfection of wisdom. The *Essence of Wisdom Sutra* is an example of the textual perfection of wisdom because it principally reveals the actual perfection of wisdom and explains the methods to attain the Wisdom Truth Body of a Buddha. Thus, in its full title the Sutra is given the name 'The perfection of wisdom', the name of that which it expresses.

This Sutra is called 'Essence' because it contains in a very few lines the essential meaning of the much longer *Perfection of Wisdom Sutras*, such as the *Perfection of Wisdom Sutra in One Hundred Thousand Lines*. The title also contains the epithet 'the Blessed Mother'. This is a translation of the Tibetan 'chom dän dä ma' (Skt. Bhagavati). The expression 'chom dän dä' is a term that is often used to refer to Buddhas. 'Chom' means 'destroyer' and signifies that a Buddha has overcome or destroyed the four maras and all faults; 'dän' means 'possessor' and indicates that Buddhas possess all good qualities; and 'dä' means 'transcended' and indicates that Buddhas have transcended sorrow. It is difficult to convey this full meaning with an English term and in general this expression has been rendered as 'Blessed One'. Although 'chom dän dä' normally refers to enlightened beings, this name is also given to the Sutra because by relying upon the teachings contained within it we can attain the final state of Buddhahood. This is an example of a cause being given the name of its effect. 'Ma' means 'mother', so the full expression 'chom dän dä ma' has been translated as 'the Blessed Mother'. This Sutra is given the name 'Mother' because the perfection of wisdom that it reveals is often called 'mother'. In general, both emptiness and the mind understanding emptiness are referred to as 'mother' because Superior beings are born from them. A Superior being (Skt. Arya) is a person who has directly realized emptiness, the ultimate nature of reality. There are four types of Superior being – the Superior Hearers and Superior Solitary Conquerors of the Hinayana lineage, and the Superior Bodhisattvas and Superior Buddhas of the Mahayana lineage. In all cases a person first becomes a Superior being by developing a direct realization of emptiness. In this sense all Superior beings are born from emptiness and the wisdom that realizes emptiness.

THE HOMAGE OF THE TRANSLATORS

Homage to the perfection of wisdom, the Blessed Mother.

Here the Tibetan translators are paying homage to the perfection of wisdom and to the enlightened being Prajnaparamita. 'The perfection of wisdom' refers principally to the resultant perfection of wisdom, which is the Wisdom Truth Body of all the Buddhas; but implicitly homage is paid also to the causal and textual perfection of wisdom. 'The Blessed Mother' here refers to Prajnaparamita, the female Buddha embodying the resultant perfection of wisdom of enlightened beings. Since the minds and bodies of enlightened beings are the same entity, the minds of Buddhas are able to manifest in physical form so that they can be perceived by other beings. When the mind that is the perfection of wisdom of the Buddhas manifests physically, it appears as Prajnaparamita. The translators made this homage at the beginning so that their work might be completed successfully and be beneficial to all beings.

Avalokiteshvara

The Background and Shariputra's Question

AN EXPLANATION OF THE MAIN BODY OF THE SUTRA

The main body of the *Essence of Wisdom Sutra* begins with an explanation of the circumstances, or background, of the Sutra, and then there follows the discourse itself. This section of the commentary is therefore divided into two principal outlines:

1 An explanation of the background to the Sutra
2 An explanation of the actual Sutra

AN EXPLANATION OF THE BACKGROUND TO THE SUTRA

This has two parts:

1 The common explanation of the background to the Sutra
2 The uncommon explanation of the background to the Sutra

THE COMMON EXPLANATION OF THE
BACKGROUND TO THE SUTRA

Thus I have heard. At one time the Blessed One was dwelling in Rajagriha on Massed Vultures Mountain together with a great assembly of monks and a great assembly of Bodhisattvas.

This part of the explanation of the background to the Sutra is called the 'common explanation' because it deals with aspects of the background that are easily understood and were commonly known by those present.

'Thus I have heard' indicates that this part of the text was explicitly spoken by Ananda, who was a close disciple of Buddha. After the passing away of Buddha it was principally Ananda who collected Buddha's words and passed on his teachings to others. Although the explanation of the background was not spoken by Buddha, these words are nevertheless considered to be the word of Buddha because Buddha himself blessed the mental continuum of Ananda and gave him permission to say this.

It is the general practice at the beginning of more extensive Sutras to present a detailed background of the Sutra. In this case the background is greatly abbreviated, but nevertheless contains the following four points:

(1) The speaker of the Sutra
(2) The time when the Sutra was delivered
(3) The place where the Sutra was delivered
(4) To whom the Sutra was spoken

THE SPEAKER OF THE SUTRA

'The Blessed One' here refers to Buddha Shakyamuni. It was he who effectively delivered this Sutra, as will be explained later.

It is very helpful to study a detailed account of the life and deeds of Buddha Shakyamuni, but here only a brief explanation will be given of his life up to the time of this Sutra. From the point of view of appearances to ordinary people, Buddha Shakyamuni attained enlightenment under the Bodhi Tree in Bodh Gaya, India, in 589 BC. In fact, at that time he was demonstrating to others how Buddhahood is attained, having already attained full enlightenment himself many aeons previously in the Pure Land known as 'Adorned with Peace and Flowers'. There he attained Buddhahood in the form of the Enjoyment Body having the name 'Buddha Munivairochana'. Having attained this state he appeared in many forms in order to benefit sentient beings throughout the universe. For the sake of those living in this particular world system he manifested as the Emanation Body known as 'Buddha Shakyamuni'.

To provide an example for those wishing to attain Buddhahood themselves, Buddha Shakyamuni carried out the twelve principal deeds that are performed by all the Buddhas who, like Buddha Shakyamuni, manifest in this world in the form of a Supreme Emanation Body. Like an ordinary being, Buddha Shakyamuni was conceived in the womb of Queen Mayadevi, the wife of King Shuddhodana of the Shakyas, and took birth as Prince Siddhartha. For the first twenty-nine years of his life he lived in his father's luxurious palace. As a boy he studied the traditional arts and sciences and showed complete mastery of all that he was taught. When he became a young man, in keeping with custom he married, and his wife, Yasodhara, later bore him a son, Rahula.

Then at the age of twenty-nine Siddhartha received many signs and predictions from the Buddhas indicating that the time had come to abandon his life as a prince and to follow the spiritual path. As a result he left the palace and, having ordained himself as a monk, spent the next six years engaged in meditation. Finally, at the age of thirty-five he showed the attainment of full enlightenment under the Bodhi Tree at Bodh Gaya.

For the first seven weeks after attaining enlightenment, as far as ordinary appearances are concerned, Buddha gave no teachings. Then Brahma and Indra appeared to him and explained that sentient beings were wandering from life to life like blind men unable to see the path that leads from suffering, sooner or later taking rebirth in the lower realms. Realizing that Buddha could not bear the suffering of others, they requested him to arise from his meditative concentration and reveal his teachings to others.

Having been entreated in this way, Buddha travelled to the Deer Park at Sarnath, near Varanasi, and there gave his first discourse, thereby turning the first Wheel of Dharma. At this time he taught the four noble truths, and through these teachings his first five disciples and many others attained personal liberation, becoming Foe Destroyers.

Thereafter Buddha travelled widely, expounding teachings of both the Hinayana and Mahayana traditions. When he was fifty-seven years old, while he was in the city of Vaishali, he was challenged by six major non-Buddhist teachers. As a result of demonstrating his extensive miracle powers Buddha overwhelmed his challengers, and many of their followers became his disciples. In this way he was able to turn the minds of many thousands of living beings towards Dharma and lead them to the state of enlightenment. After demonstrating his powers at Vaishali, Buddha travelled to Rajagriha, and it was near that town that he expounded the *Perfection of Wisdom Sutras*.

THE TIME WHEN THE SUTRA WAS DELIVERED

'At one time' refers to the period after Buddha had travelled to Rajagriha from Vaishali, having given the demonstration of his extensive miracle powers mentioned above. Buddha was therefore about fifty-seven years old when he delivered this Sutra.

THE PLACE WHERE THE SUTRA WAS DELIVERED

'Was dwelling in Rajagriha on Massed Vultures Mountain': this Sutra, as well as the longer *Perfection of Wisdom Sutras*, was delivered while Buddha Shakyamuni was staying near Rajagriha, which is in the present day Bihar province of India, quite near to Bodh Gaya. The precise location of the discourse was a mountain known as 'Massed Vultures Mountain' (Skt. Gridhrakutaparvata).

When Buddha was expounding the *Perfection of Wisdom Sutras* many Bodhisattvas from various world systems came to listen, manifesting in the form of vultures. To the eyes of ordinary people it appeared that the mountain was covered in a vast flock of vultures, and as a result the mountain became known as 'Massed Vultures Mountain'. This is one of several interpretations of the origin of this name.

TO WHOM THE SUTRA WAS SPOKEN

'Together with a great assembly of monks and a great assembly of Bodhisattvas': since Buddha was giving Mahayana discourses during his time on Massed Vultures Mountain, his circle of followers included not only a great number of monks (Skt. bhikshu), such as Shariputra and Subhuti, but also a great number of Bodhisattvas, such as Avalokiteshvara and Maitreya.

THE UNCOMMON EXPLANATION OF THE BACKGROUND TO THE SUTRA

At that time the Blessed One was absorbed in the concentration of the countless aspects of phenomena, called 'Profound Illumination'.

At that time also the Superior Avalokiteshvara, the Bodhisattva, the Great Being, was looking perfectly at the practice of the profound perfection of wisdom, looking perfectly at the emptiness of inherent existence also of the five aggregates.

This part of the explanation of the background to the Sutra is called the 'uncommon explanation' because it explains aspects of the circumstances of the Sutra that were not commonly known by those present.

At the time of the Sutra, which was during his stay on Massed Vultures Mountain, Buddha was absorbed in a state of meditative concentration on the emptiness, or ultimate nature, of the countless aspects of all phenomena. This meditative concentration is called 'Profound Illumination' because while Buddha's mind was focused single-pointedly on the profound object, emptiness, his body radiated a vast amount of brilliant light, filling the entire world. The light purified the environment and sentient beings' minds, and caused the seeds of the paths to liberation and full enlightenment to ripen in their minds. Only those beings with sufficiently pure minds were able to perceive that Buddha was engaged in this practice and emanating light in this way. That is why this part of the background is included in the uncommon explanation.

There was another reason why Buddha radiated light in this way. When profound discourses such as the *Perfection of Wisdom Sutras* were being given, a vast host of gods from the desire and form realms also came to listen. These gods have bodies that radiate light, and from their point of view humans are stunted, bad-smelling, and toad-like. Therefore, when these celestial beings took their places about Massed Vultures Mountain their minds were filled with haughtiness and pride. Having such pride is a great obstacle to receiving benefit from spiritual teachings and so to deflate their pride Buddha radiated brilliant light from his own body. His body outshone those of the gods as the sun outshines the light of fireflies. Through this display the gods were humbled and their minds became receptive to Buddha's teachings.

While Buddha was absorbed in concentration, Avaloki-teshvara was meditating on the profound view of empti-ness. In the text it states specifically that Avalokiteshvara was observing how the five aggregates are empty of inher-ent existence, but the presence of the word 'also' implies that Avalokiteshvara had also looked at the emptiness of inherent existence of the self, or person. What is meant by 'emptiness of inherent existence' will be explained in the next chapter.

The special qualities of Avalokiteshvara are indicated by the references to him as 'the Superior Avalokiteshvara, the Bodhisattva, the Great Being'. He is given the title 'Super-ior' because he has realized emptiness directly and is thus a Superior being. Avalokiteshvara is also a Bodhisattva, a person who is continuously and spontaneously motivated by the mind of enlightenment (Skt. bodhichitta). Someone who has developed this motivation has thereby entered the Mahayana path. Bodhichitta has two principal aspirations: the wish to benefit and bring happiness to all sentient beings without exception, and the wish to attain the state of Buddhahood in order to be most able to accomplish the first aspiration. A Bodhisattva is therefore someone who is prin-cipally motivated by these two wishes. Avalokiteshvara is worthy to be called a 'Great Being' (Skt. Mahasattva) because, being a Bodhisattva, he works with great courage and energy solely for the benefit and welfare of others.

Although he assumed the form of a Bodhisattva disciple of Buddha Shakyamuni, Avalokiteshvara had already attained full enlightenment many aeons previously. The same is also true of Manjushri, Vajrapani, Samantabhadra,

Maitreya, and the other principal Mahayana followers of Buddha Shakyamuni. Although they were in essence Buddhas themselves, they demonstrated the correct manner of being Bodhisattva disciples and helped to spread the teachings of Buddha Shakyamuni in order to benefit others extensively.

AN EXPLANATION OF THE ACTUAL SUTRA

The part of the text considered so far, giving the background to the actual discourse, is omitted from some shorter versions of the Sutra. The remaining part of the text contains the actual Sutra and is explained in four parts:

1 The question of Shariputra
2 The answers by Avalokiteshvara
3 The approval of the answers by Buddha
4 The followers are pleased and take the teachings to heart

THE QUESTION OF SHARIPUTRA

Then, through the power of Buddha, the Venerable Shariputra said to the Superior Avalokiteshvara, the Bodhisattva, the Great Being, 'How should a Son of the lineage train who wishes to engage in the practice of the profound perfection of wisdom?'

This part of the Sutra consists of a question by Shariputra addressed to Avalokiteshvara. While Buddha was absorbed in the meditative concentration called 'Profound Illumination' he blessed the minds of Shariputra and Avalokiteshvara so that Shariputra was inspired to ask his question and Avalokiteshvara was inspired to give his answers. Therefore, since both disciples spoke through the power and inspiration of Buddha, the entire Sutra is correctly considered to be the word of Buddha.

If something is the word of Buddha it is not necessarily spoken through the mouth of Buddha. For example, in some Sutras Buddha gave teachings through his crown protrusion, and in one Sutra, through the power of Buddha, even the wind moving the branches of a tree gave rise to words of Dharma. Those Sutras, as well as this present Sutra, are the authentic word of Buddha because they arose through Buddha's power and inspiration.

Shariputra was one of the main disciples of Buddha Shakyamuni, having a very special relationship with him from previous lives. From the point of view of ordinary appearances he was a Hearer Foe Destroyer of the Hinayana lineage.

In Shariputra's question, 'Son of the lineage' refers to someone who has entered the Mahayana lineage. A person enters the Mahayana lineage by developing the mind of great compassion, so Shariputra is referring to someone who has cultivated this mind. Although Shariputra refers only to 'Son' of the lineage in his question, 'Daughter' of the lineage is also implied, and is expressed explicitly in the answer given by Avalokiteshvara. Indeed, some texts also contain the word 'Daughter' at this point.

Here, the phrase 'the practice of the profound perfection of wisdom' refers to emptiness. In effect, emptiness is being called 'profound', 'the perfection of wisdom', and 'the object to be practised'. Emptiness is called 'profound' because if we realize emptiness we shall be able to accomplish the great purpose of attaining liberation from cyclic existence (Skt. samsara). Emptiness is called 'the perfection of wisdom' because emptiness is the main object of the actual perfection of wisdom. Emptiness is also called 'the object to be practised' because the practice of emptiness is indispensable if we wish to attain liberation. Without the complete realization of emptiness we cannot attain even the liberation of a Hinayana Hearer, and certainly without this realization we cannot accomplish the final attainment of Buddhahood.

The meaning of Shariputra's question is therefore, 'How should someone who has developed great compassion train, if he or she wishes to engage in the practice of emptiness?'

Manjushri

The Paths of Accumulation and Preparation (1)

THE ANSWERS BY AVALOKITESHVARA

The next section of the Sutra consists of the answers given by Avalokiteshvara to the question of Shariputra. This section has three parts:

1 The answer intended for those with minds of lower faculties
2 The answer intended for those with minds of higher faculties
3 The exhortation to practise the perfection of wisdom

THE ANSWER INTENDED FOR THOSE WITH MINDS OF LOWER FACULTIES

The parts of Avalokiteshvara's answer included in this outline are more explicit and easier to understand than the later part of his answer intended for those with higher faculties. Nevertheless, his answer reveals very subtle and profound meanings, and is not easily understood without a commentary and careful study.

Avalokiteshvara's answers to Shariputra's question explain how to practise the perfection of wisdom in relation to the five Mahayana paths. Therefore at this point it will be helpful to consider the meaning of paths in general, and the five Mahayana paths in particular.

In general, there are two types of path – external paths and internal paths. We are all familiar with external paths. These lead from one external place to another and we can easily understand them by consulting maps and so forth. Internal paths, on the other hand, are types of mind and are much more difficult to understand. Although internal paths are minds, they are called 'paths' because they lead to particular destinations, or effects. Those types of mind that lead to rebirth in samsara are mundane paths. Some of these paths are non-virtuous, leading to rebirth in the three lower realms, and others are virtuous, leading to rebirth in the three higher realms. Minds that lead to complete liberation from samsara are supramundane paths, and can be divided into Hinayana paths, which lead to personal liberation, and Mahayana paths, which lead to the full enlightenment of Buddhahood. Hinayana paths include the five paths of the Solitary Conqueror and the five paths of the Hearer. Similarly, there are five Mahayana paths – the Mahayana paths of accumulation, preparation, seeing, meditation, and No More Learning. These five Mahayana paths are minds that lead progressively to the attainment of full enlightenment – the fifth Mahayana path being the fully enlightened mind itself. The way to enter the Mahayana

paths and to progress from path to path will be described in
the course of this commentary.

Avalokiteshvara's explanation of how to practise the perfection of wisdom in relation to the five Mahayana paths
has five parts:

1 A brief explanation of how to practise the
perfection of wisdom on the paths of
accumulation and preparation
2 An extensive explanation of how to practise
the perfection of wisdom on the paths of
accumulation and preparation
3 An explanation of how to practise the perfection
of wisdom on the path of seeing
4 An explanation of how to practise the perfection
of wisdom on the path of meditation
5 An explanation of how to attain the Path of No
More Learning

A BRIEF EXPLANATION OF HOW TO PRACTISE THE PERFECTION OF WISDOM ON THE PATHS OF ACCUMULATION AND PREPARATION

**Thus he spoke, and the Superior Avalokiteshvara, the
Bodhisattva, the Great Being, replied to the Venerable
Shariputra as follows:**

**'Shariputra, whatever Son or Daughter of the lin-
eage wishes to engage in the practice of the profound
perfection of wisdom should look perfectly like this:
subsequently looking perfectly and correctly at the
emptiness of inherent existence also of the five
aggregates.'**

After Shariputra had asked his question, Avalokiteshvara was inspired through the power of Buddha to deliver his answer. In his reply Avalokiteshvara refers to 'whatever Son or Daughter of the lineage wishes to engage in the practice of the profound perfection of wisdom'. The wording echoes the question of Shariputra, but here 'Daughter' of the lineage is included explicitly, making it clear that the advice that follows applies to both male and female practitioners. Avalokiteshvara's advice is that the practitioner 'should look ... at the emptiness of inherent existence also of the five aggregates.'

The five aggregates, which are discussed more fully under the next outline, are categories into which all impermanent phenomena can be divided; and in particular the constituents of a person can be divided into these five aggregates. The emptiness of inherent existence of the five aggregates is the aggregates' ultimate nature, since ultimately the five aggregates lack, or are empty of, inherent existence. The meaning of emptiness and inherent existence are explained later in this chapter.

The presence of the word 'also' in Avalokiteshvara's answer implies that a Son or Daughter of the lineage should also look perfectly at the emptiness of inherent existence of the person, or self. Each living being can be considered as an individual person, and this person who is composed of five aggregates is, like the aggregates themselves, also empty of inherent existence.

Avalokiteshvara describes the manner in which we should look at the emptiness of inherent existence of the five aggregates as 'perfectly like this: subsequently looking perfectly and correctly'. Here the word 'subsequently' has great meaning. It indicates that the mind with which we should first understand emptiness is an inferential cognizer, the Tibetan expression for an inferential cognizer being rendered more literally as 'subsequent realization'.

An inferential cognizer is a type of valid mind, or valid cognizer – a valid cognizer being a mind that realizes its object non-deceptively. Such a mind will never deceive us with respect to the object it ascertains. There are two types of valid cognizer: inferential valid cognizers and direct valid cognizers. They are distinguished by the fact that an inferential valid cognizer relies upon a sign, or reason, to know its object, whereas a direct valid cognizer knows its object directly without the need to rely upon a reason.

We have a lot of experience of direct valid cognizers as this category of mind includes all valid sense consciousnesses. For example, the eye consciousness that correctly ascertains this book is a direct valid cognizer because it ascertains the book directly without any reasoning. Inferential valid cognizers are less common but they are an important form of understanding. We can consider a simple example. When we see smoke rising from the chimney of a house we may develop the certainty that a fire has been lit in that house. We cannot see the fire directly, but using the presence of the smoke as a sign, or reason, we know without a doubt that there is (or has been) a fire. Therefore, smoke is a correct sign indicating the existence of fire, and the mind that realizes the existence of fire in dependence upon this sign is an inferential valid cognizer. Also, we can sometimes know that a person is unhappy by seeing him or her crying. Although we cannot see the person's state of mind directly, we develop an inferential cognizer that knows the person is unhappy by using the outward behaviour as a sign. Since an inferential cognizer depends upon a reason we must first develop a realization of the reason before we can generate the inferential cognizer, which is why the Tibetan expression for an inferential cognizer is more literally 'subsequent realization'. For example, we must first see smoke and then subsequently we can develop the inferential cognizer that realizes there is a fire.

Not all minds are valid cognizers because not all minds know their object non-deceptively. For example, a tree stump at dusk may appear to our eye consciousness as a person, but this mind is not a valid mind and deceives us. Also a child may develop the thought that certain berries are good to eat because they are black and shiny. This thought is similar to an inferential cognizer but it is not a valid mind because the reason used is not correct. The resulting mind is deceptive and could even lead to the child's death.

If we wish to gain faultless knowledge of a phenomenon we must know that phenomenon with a valid cognizer. There are many phenomena we can know immediately by direct valid cognizers simply by seeing them, hearing them, smelling them, and so forth. Such objects are called 'manifest objects'. Other phenomena such as atoms and events that occurred before our birth are hidden objects for us. At present we cannot gain knowledge of these phenomena directly, but, nevertheless, we can know them correctly with inferential valid cognizers in dependence upon signs or reasons. Likewise, emptiness is a hidden object and initially cannot be realized directly. First we must gain a correct understanding of the reasons that indicate emptiness, and then subsequently through contemplating these reasons we can gain an inferential realization of emptiness.

This section of the Sutra therefore explains briefly how to practise the perfection of wisdom by generating an inferential realization of emptiness. Among those who have entered the Mahayana path, only those on the Mahayana paths of accumulation and preparation realize emptiness inferentially in this way, since practitioners on higher paths realize emptiness directly by means of a non-conceptual mind. Thus, the answer given by Avalokiteshvara in this section of the Sutra explains the practice of the perfection of wisdom on the Mahayana paths of accumulation and preparation.

We enter the Mahayana path of accumulation, the first of the five paths, when we develop non-fabricated, or spontaneous, bodhichitta, and thereby become a Bodhisattva. Although Bodhisattvas on both the path of accumulation and the second path, the path of preparation, realize emptiness with inferential valid cognizers, there is a difference in the strength of their realizations of emptiness. This can be understood in terms of the three wisdoms.

Inferential cognizers realizing emptiness have the nature of wisdom and can be of three types: wisdom arisen from listening, wisdom arisen from contemplation, and wisdom arisen from meditation. The first of these, wisdom arisen from listening, is an inferential cognizer realizing emptiness that arises in dependence principally upon reasons that are established and explained by others. If we have very strong imprints from previous lives, it is possible to realize emptiness without receiving instructions from others in this life, but generally we all need to listen to or read teachings on emptiness before we can gain a realization of it. Therefore for most people the mind that first realizes emptiness is wisdom arisen from listening. After having realized emptiness in this way, if we continue to contemplate and meditate we can gain a more powerful realization of emptiness in dependence upon reasons established through our own contemplation. This is wisdom arisen from contemplation. Having developed this, if we continue to meditate on emptiness we gain a special valid experience of emptiness through the power of meditation. This special understanding is wisdom arisen from meditation. Although these three wisdoms all realize the same object, emptiness, there is a difference in their strength and how they arise. Wisdom arisen from meditation is more powerful than wisdom arisen from contemplation, which in turn is more powerful than wisdom arisen from listening.

Bodhisattvas on the path of accumulation improve their realization of emptiness by depending principally upon wisdom arisen from listening and wisdom arisen from contemplation. Bodhisattvas on this path have already attained tranquil abiding – a very supple, single-pointed concentration – since without tranquil abiding it is not possible to attain the perfect, non-fabricated mind of enlightenment that is the gateway to the Mahayana paths. With their tranquil abiding concentration they meditate on emptiness. Bodhisattvas on the path of accumulation are able to generate the wisdoms arisen from listening and from contemplation, but they are not able to generate the wisdom arisen from meditation observing emptiness. This last wisdom is the mind of superior seeing observing emptiness and is not possessed by Bodhisattvas on the path of accumulation.

Superior seeing observing emptiness develops out of the experience of meditating on emptiness with tranquil abiding. It is attained when the meditator attains a special suppleness induced by wisdom. The mind of superior seeing can investigate emptiness while at the same time remaining in single-pointed concentration on emptiness. Just as a small fish can swim in a still lake without disturbing the surface of the water, the mind of superior seeing can investigate emptiness without disturbing the concentration of tranquil abiding on emptiness.

The moment a Bodhisattva attains superior seeing observing emptiness, he or she has at that very moment attained the Mahayana path of preparation; and thus superior seeing observing emptiness is possessed by a Bodhisattva on the path of preparation but not by a Bodhisattva on the path of accumulation. Having attained the path of preparation, Bodhisattvas continue to enhance their practice of the perfection of wisdom by depending upon superior seeing observing emptiness – this being the wisdom arisen from meditation observing emptiness. Thus, although Bodhisattvas on both the paths of accumulation and preparation realize emptiness by means of inferential cognizers, there are differences in the type of wisdom that observes emptiness on these two paths.

In summary, this part of Avalokiteshvara's answer explains that if we are a Mahayana practitioner wishing to develop the perfection of wisdom we should meditate on the emptiness of inherent existence of the five aggregates and of persons. While on the path of accumulation we should enhance our understanding of emptiness by relying principally upon the wisdoms arisen from listening and contemplation. By strengthening our experience of emptiness we shall develop superior seeing observing emptiness and progress to the path of preparation. On this path we should continue to meditate on emptiness by relying upon the wisdom arisen from meditation.

AN EXTENSIVE EXPLANATION OF HOW TO PRACTISE THE PERFECTION OF WISDOM ON THE PATHS OF ACCUMULATION AND PREPARATION

In the previous section of the Sutra Avalokiteshvara gave a brief explanation of how to practise the perfection of wisdom while on the Mahayana paths of accumulation and preparation. The next part of his answer explains this practice in more detail, and is considered under two outlines:

1 The meditation on the four profundities of the aggregate of form
2 The meditation on the four profundities of the aggregates of feeling and so forth

THE MEDITATION ON THE FOUR PROFUNDITIES OF
THE AGGREGATE OF FORM

Avalokiteshvara first presents the four profundities of form. The four profundities are:

(1) The profundity of the ultimate
(2) The profundity of the conventional
(3) The profundity of the two truths being the same entity
(4) The profundity of the two truths being nominally distinct

This part of his answer is therefore discussed under four outlines:

1 The meditation on the first profundity of the aggregate of form
2 The meditation on the second profundity of the aggregate of form
3 The meditation on the third profundity of the aggregate of form
4 The meditation on the fourth profundity of the aggregate of form

THE MEDITATION ON THE FIRST PROFUNDITY OF THE
AGGREGATE OF FORM

'Form is empty'

The first profundity is the emptiness of inherent existence of phenomena. It is called a 'profundity' because emptiness is a profound topic that is difficult to realize and because

the realization of emptiness leads to the profound attainment of complete liberation from all suffering. It is called
the 'profundity of the ultimate' because emptiness is the
ultimate nature of phenomena.

Avalokiteshvara's words 'form is empty' reveal the ultimate nature of form and thus they reveal the first profundity of form. 'Form', here, refers to the aggregate of form,
which is one of the five aggregates. The five aggregates are:

(1) The aggregate of form
(2) The aggregate of feeling
(3) The aggregate of discrimination
(4) The aggregate of compositional factors
(5) The aggregate of consciousness

In general, the five aggregates include all impermanent
phenomena – any impermanent phenomenon can be included in one of the five. The five aggregates of a person
include the particular impermanent phenomena that constitute the person.

The aggregate of form includes all the objects of the five
sense consciousnesses – everything that our eyes can see,
our ears can hear, our nose can smell, our tongue can taste,
and our body can sense or touch. All gross physical objects
such as mountains, tables, and books, as well as all colours
and shapes, sounds, smells, tastes, and tactile objects are
therefore included in the aggregate of form. The aggregate
of form of a person is the person's body, together with its
colour, shape, and so forth.

The aggregate of feeling comprises a particular type of
mind, namely the mental factor feeling. Feeling is an

example of an all-accompanying mental factor, which means that it is a mental factor that accompanies every moment of consciousness. When a primary mind comes into contact with its object, feeling functions to experience the object as pleasant, unpleasant, or neutral. There are therefore three types of feeling: pleasant feelings, unpleasant feelings, and neutral feelings. The aggregate of feeling of a person is the mental factor feeling within the continuum of the person's mind.

The aggregate of discrimination includes all examples of the mental factor discrimination. Like feeling, discrimination is a mental factor that accompanies every moment of mind. It enables us to distinguish one object from another, right from wrong, and so forth, in dependence upon the particular characteristics, or signs, of an object. The aggregate of discrimination of a person is the mental factor discrimination within the continuum of the person's mind.

The aggregate of compositional factors comprises two types of phenomenon: mental factors and non-associated compounded phenomena. In total there are fifty-one mental factors, and all except feeling and discrimination are included in the aggregate of compositional factors. This aggregate includes the other all-accompanying mental factors – attention, intention, and contact; virtuous mental factors such as faith and effort; mental factors that are delusions such as anger and jealousy; and other types of mental factor such as mindfulness and regret. Non-associated compounded phenomena include all impermanent phenomena that are neither form nor mind, such as persons, life, time, and potentialities. Persons are included in this category because although a person has a mind and has form, the phenomenon, person, is itself neither mind nor form, yet it is impermanent. The aggregate of compositional factors of a person includes all the compositional factors within the continuum of the person.

The aggregate of consciousness includes the six primary minds, namely eye consciousness, ear consciousness, nose consciousness, tongue consciousness, body consciousness, and mental consciousness. The aggregate of consciousness of a person is the six primary minds within the continuum of the person.

In this Sutra the aggregate of form is taken as the first basis for establishing emptiness. Also, in the *Perfection of Wisdom Sutra in One Hundred Thousand Lines*, in which one hundred and eight objects of knowledge from form to omniscience are taken as bases for establishing emptiness, form is taken as the first basis. Once we have realized emptiness using one basis, such as form, it is not difficult to establish the emptiness of other phenomena.

Emptiness is interpreted somewhat differently in the various Buddhist schools. The presentation given here is in accordance with the Madhyamika-Prasangika system of tenets, which is the ultimate view of Buddha as expounded in the *Perfection of Wisdom Sutras*. Buddha taught different philosophical systems according to the various needs and capabilities of his followers, but his intention was to lead all living beings eventually to the final view of the Madhyamika-Prasangika school. There is no higher view than this.

According to the Madhyamika-Prasangika school, emptiness is emptiness of inherent existence. Thus, when

Avalokiteshvara says that form 'is empty', he means that form is empty of inherent existence, or that form does not exist inherently. To understand the significance of this it is necessary to understand the meaning of inherent existence. We need to understand what would be the characteristics of an object if it existed inherently.

If something were inherently existent it would have an existence within itself, independent of other phenomena. According to the Madhyamika-Prasangika school, if an object were inherently existent it would also be truly existent and existent from its own side. An object is truly existent if it exists truly as it appears and can be found upon investigation. Something exists from its own side if its existence is established from the side of the object itself without depending upon an apprehending consciousness.

If we are ordinary beings, all objects appear to us to exist inherently. Objects seem to be independent of our mind and independent of other phenomena. The universe appears to consist of discrete objects that have an existence from their own side. These objects appear to exist in themselves as stars, planets, mountains, people, and so forth, 'waiting' to be experienced by conscious beings. Normally it does not occur to us that we are involved in any way in the existence of these phenomena. Instead, each object appears to have an existence completely independent of us and all other objects.

With his words 'form is empty' Avalokiteshvara is saying that although objects that are included in the aggregate of form appear to exist inherently in this way, in reality they totally lack inherent existence. The way in which these

objects actually exist is quite different from the way in
which they appear to exist.

The question of whether objects exist inherently or not
is extremely important because all our sufferings and dissatisfaction can be traced to our clinging to the inherent
existence of ourself and other phenomena. It is necessary
to realize that phenomena lack inherent existence in order
to gain liberation from suffering and to attain full
enlightenment.

Until we attain the path of seeing we need to rely upon
logical reasons to realize emptiness. This Sutra does not
explicitly explain the reasons that demonstrate the emptiness of inherent existence of form, but many reasons are
given in the longer *Perfection of Wisdom Sutras*. These reasons can be extracted and used here. The explanations of
emptiness given in the *Perfection of Wisdom Sutra in One
Hundred Thousand Lines* are condensed in the two shorter
Perfection of Wisdom Sutras containing twenty-five thousand
and eight thousand lines, and also in the *Condensed Perfection of Wisdom Sutra*. Although the explanations are condensed in the shorter Sutras, all the essential reasons given
in the extensive Sutra are retained.

In the *Condensed Perfection of Wisdom Sutra* Buddha says
that form and the other aggregates are empty of inherent
existence because just as the depth of the ocean cannot be
measured by shooting an arrow, if we investigate the aggregates with wisdom we cannot find them. It is clear that if
we were to shoot an arrow into the ocean we could not discover the depth of the ocean in this way. Similarly, if we
investigate the aggregates using sharp wisdom we shall not

find anything that we can point to and say, 'This is the aggregate of form', and so forth. If we are not content to accept the mere name 'aggregates' but instead try to discover the aggregates themselves, we shall be unable to find them. The fact that the aggregates cannot be found when investigated with wisdom is a reason used by Buddha to show that the aggregates lack inherent existence.

Our inability to find form upon analytical investigation can therefore be used to demonstrate that form is empty. We can take our body as an example of the aggregate of form to illustrate how the reason may be applied. If we are ordinary beings, at present we have a view of our body as being inherently existent. Our body seems to be a single entity independent of the rest of the universe, and does not seem to rely upon any conceptual process for its existence – it appears to us to be a solid, discrete object existing under its own power. Viewing our body in this way, we cherish it and react accordingly to cold, hunger, gentle caresses, and so forth.

If our body really were inherently existent as it appears to be, we would expect to be able to find it upon investigation. This follows because our body would exist under its own power, independently of other phenomena, and therefore we could physically or mentally remove all objects that are not our body, and our body would still remain, existing by itself. Therefore, if we have an inherently existent body we should be able to point to our body without pointing to any phenomenon that is not our body.

We can check to see whether we can find our body in this way. If we wish to point to our body, what do we point to?

We may point to the centre of our body, around our chest, or we may point to our head, arm, leg, and so on. If when we point to our chest we are pointing to our body, it follows that our chest must be our body. If this is so, then equally our head must be our body, our arm must be our body, and so forth. It is clear that these objects are parts of our body, but are they each our body itself? If they are, it follows that we have many bodies since there are many parts of the body. This is obviously nonsense. Alternatively, since we have only one body, if the parts of our body are our body itself, it follows that the parts of our body are a single object. This also is nonsense. We must conclude that when we point to a part of our body such as our chest we are pointing to a phenomenon that is not our body itself. We can be sure, therefore, that upon investigation we cannot find our body among its individual parts.

As we continue to search for our body we may think that the collection of the various parts of our body is our body. We may feel that when we point to the collection of our chest, head, arms, and so forth, we have found our body. We need to investigate this possibility carefully. We have already established that each individual part of our body is not our body. The collection of the parts of our body is therefore a collection of objects that are not a body. We can say it is a collection of 'non-bodies'. It is impossible for the mere collection of non-bodies to be a body, just as it is impossible for a collection of non-sheep, for example goats, to be sheep. Since a collection of sheep is sheep and a collection of books is books, it follows that a collection of non-bodies is non-bodies and cannot possibly be a body. We can conclude that the collection of parts of our body is parts of our body, but it is not our body itself.

There is another way in which we can know that the collection of the parts of our body is not our body. If we can point to the collection of the parts of our body and say that this, in itself, is our body, then the collection of the parts of our body must exist independently of all phenomena that are not our body, so it would follow that the collection of the parts of our body exists independently of the parts themselves. This is clearly absurd – if it were true we could remove all the parts of our body and the collection of the parts would remain. Again we can conclude that the collection of the parts of our body cannot be identified as our body itself.

So far we have been unable to find our body among the parts of our body or the collection of the parts of our body. The only remaining place to find our body is completely separate from the parts of our body. If our body existed in such a way we could remove all the parts of our body and our body would still remain. Quite clearly this is not the case. We must conclude that we cannot find anything separate from the parts of our body that we can point to as our body.

We have now considered all possible places where we can find our body and have failed to locate it. If our body really does exist inherently as it appears to, we must be able to find it by isolating it from all other phenomena. Since we cannot succeed in doing this, we can come to the firm conclusion that our body is empty of inherent existence.

Unless we investigate in this way we naturally have the view that we have a body that has its own independent existence. We feel that we can see and point to this self-existing body. However, whenever we see or point to our body we are seeing and pointing to parts of our body. We should investigate this point carefully. When we say we see our body, what in fact do we see? We see only the parts of our body – our arms, legs, and so forth. When we look at our body there is nothing that we see that is not a part of our body, and if something is a part of our body it is necessarily not our body. As already pointed out, if each part of our body were our body it would follow that we have many bodies. We may propose that the collection of the parts of our body is our body, but the collection of the parts of our body is still just parts of our body. When we see the collection of the parts of our body we see only parts of our body.

If we apprehend a body that is other than the parts of the body, that body is what is called the 'inherently existent body'. This is the negated object of the emptiness of our body. However hard we search we shall never find such a body. When we look for our body we perceive only the parts of our body. Other than these parts there is no body to be found.

When we search for our body we are unable to find it. We may think that although we cannot find our body itself, at least we can find its parts – the head, the arms, and so forth. However, if we investigate more carefully, taking our head as an example, we again experience difficulty in finding the object of our investigation. When we try to point to our head we point to our nose, eyes, cheek, and so forth. The same arguments that were used to show that the parts of our body are not our body can be used to demonstrate that these parts of our head are not our head. Similarly, the collection of the parts of our head is not our head, nor can our head be found anywhere else. In this way we can realize that our head does not exist inherently. We can apply the same reasoning to demonstrate that our nose, the living cells of our nose, and even the molecules and atoms making up the cells are all empty of inherent existence.

The emptiness of our body and its parts can be illustrated by considering the example of a toy snake. If someone places a toy rubber snake in our room, the first time we see it we may believe that it is a real snake and be quite startled by it. Even though there is no actual snake in our room, a snake appears vividly to our mind. For a short time we may cling to this appearance as real and develop fear as a result. However, if we look more carefully we shall discover that the snake does not exist in the way that it appears. Clearly there is no real snake existing from its own side; we have merely imputed a snake with our conceptual mind. Apart from the mere appearance of a snake to our mind, there is no real snake to be found anywhere in our room. When we realize this, all our fears associated with the snake immediately subside.

If we check carefully, we discover that our body and the snake that appears to our mind in the example above exist in a very similar way. Just like the snake, our body appears vividly to our mind and seems to exist from its own side. However, as with the snake, if we investigate we are unable to find our body and we discover that it has no existence of its own but is merely imputed by our mind. Like the snake, our body is a mere appearance to our mind. As long as we believe that it has its own inherent existence our body can be a source of fear and pain, but when we realize that it is merely imputed by our mind these fears and so forth will decrease and eventually disappear, just as our fear of the snake is overcome when we realize that it is only imputed.

Although the snake and our body exist in a very similar way, there is an important difference. When we discover that the snake is really a toy snake and realize that the real snake was merely imputed by our mind, we conclude that a real snake does not exist at all in our room. However, when we realize that our body is merely imputed by our mind it would be a great mistake to conclude that our body does not exist at all. It is true that the inherently existent body that normally appears to our mind has no more existence than the real snake that appears to be in our room – both are completely non-existent. Nevertheless, a body that is empty of inherent existence and is merely imputed upon the collection of the parts of our body does exist. A merely imputed body exists because the parts of our body are, by convention, a suitable basis upon which to impute a body because they can perform the functions of a body. A length of striped rubber, on the other hand, is not a suitable basis upon which to impute a real snake because it cannot perform the functions of a snake. Therefore, in the example described above, we say that a real snake does not exist at all in our room. Both the snake and our body are merely imputed by our mind, but our body is imputed correctly whereas the snake is imputed incorrectly. To overcome the sufferings associated with our body we need to accept the body that is merely imputed upon a valid basis and abandon the conceptual mind that clings to an inherently existent body.

Another example that is often used to illustrate the meaning of emptiness is the experience of dreaming. When we dream, we may have extremely vivid experiences. We may travel to colourful lands, meet beautiful or terrifying people, engage in various activities, and as a result experience great pleasure or suffering and pain. In our dream a whole world appears to us, functioning in its own way. This world may be similar to the world of our waking state or it may be quite bizarre, but in either case while we are dreaming it appears to be utterly real. It is quite rare to have the slightest suspicion that what we are experiencing is just a dream. The world we inhabit in our dream seems to have its own existence completely independent of our mind, and we respond to the world in our normal way, with desire, anger, fear, and so on.

If, while we are still dreaming, we try to test whether the world we are experiencing is real or not, for example by tapping the objects around us or by questioning the other people in our dream, we shall probably get a response that seems to confirm the reality of our dream surroundings. In fact, the only certain way to know that we have been dreaming is to wake up. Then we instantly realize without any doubt that the world we were experiencing in our dream was deceptive and was merely an appearance to our mind. It is quite clear once we are awake that what we experience in a dream does not exist from its own side but

Vajrapani

depends completely upon our mind. For example, if we dream of an elephant, the 'dream elephant' is merely an appearance to our mind and cannot be found inside our bedroom or elsewhere.

If we check carefully, we shall realize that our waking world exists in a way that is similar to the way in which our dream world exists. Like the dream world, our waking world appears vividly to us and seems to have its own existence independent of our mind. Just as in the dream, we believe this appearance to be true and respond with desire, anger, fear, and so on. Also, if we superficially test our waking world as we did our dream world to see whether it really does exist in the way that it appears, we shall again receive an apparent confirmation of our view. If we tap the objects around us they will appear to be quite solid and real, and if we ask other people they will say that they are seeing the same objects in the same way as we do. However, we should not take this apparent confirmation of the inherent existence of objects as conclusive, since we know that similar tests cannot reveal the actual nature of our dream world. To understand the true nature of our waking world we must investigate and meditate deeply, using the type of analysis already described. When by these means we realize emptiness we shall understand that objects such as our body do not exist from their own side. Like the dream elephant they are mere appearances to our mind. Nevertheless our world functions, following its own apparent rules in accordance with the laws of cause and effect, just as our dream world functions in its own way.

The experience of realizing emptiness can therefore be compared to waking up. Once we realize emptiness we see clearly and without any doubt that the world as we experienced it before was deceptive and false. It appeared to have its own inherent existence, but having understood emptiness we realize that it is completely empty of inherent existence and depends upon our mind. In fact, Buddha is sometimes called the 'Awakened One' because he has awakened from the 'sleep' of ignorance.

In Buddha's scriptures, emptiness of inherent existence is often compared to space. We say that we see space, but we do not normally check what kind of space we are seeing; we are satisfied with just the name 'space'. If we investigate to find out what we are actually seeing when we say we see space we shall not be able find anything – it is just empty. Similarly, if we are not satisfied with the mere name 'my body' but try to find out what kind of body we see, we shall discover that we cannot see our body at all. Our body is also empty – empty of inherent existence.

Although we talk about empty space, the emptiness of space that we normally refer to is not the same as the emptiness of our body. However, empty space is the best example to help us to understand the meaning of profound emptiness. To benefit from this example we need to understand clearly the meaning of space (Tib. nam kha).

There are two principal types of space: produced space and unproduced space. Produced space is the visible space that we can see inside a room or in the sky. This space may become dark at night and light during the day, and because it undergoes change in this way it is an impermanent phenomenon and can be seen with our eyes. The character-istic property of produced space is that it does not obstruct objects. For example, if there is space in a room we can place objects there without obstruction. Similarly birds are able to fly through the space of the sky because it lacks obstruction, whereas they cannot fly through a mountain! Therefore, we can say that produced space lacks, or is empty of, obstructive contact. This mere lack, or emptiness, of obstructive contact is unproduced space. Since unpro-duced space is the mere absence of obstructive contact it does not undergo momentary change and is therefore a per-manent phenomenon. Whereas produced space is visible and quite easy to know, unproduced space is a mere absence and is rather more subtle. However, once we understand unproduced space we shall find it easier to understand emptiness.

Unproduced space is a negative phenomenon. A negative phenomenon is a phenomenon that is realized through the explicit elimination of the phenomenon's object of negation by the mind that apprehends the phenomenon. In the case of unproduced space the object of negation is obstructive contact, and space is realized by a mind that explicitly elim-inates this object of negation. Furthermore, unproduced space is a non-affirming negative, which means that unpro-duced space is realized by a mind through its elimination of the object of negation without that mind realizing another positive object. The mind that realizes unproduced space negates obstructive contact but does not affirm any other phenomenon. In contrast, some phenomena are affirming negatives. An affirming negative is a phenomenon that is

realized by a mind that explicitly eliminates the phenomenon's object of negation and that indirectly realizes a positive phenomenon. An example of an affirming negative is
my cousin's lack of being female, since the mind that realizes my cousin's lack of being female indirectly realizes that
my cousin is male. On the other hand, unproduced space
does not imply any positive phenomenon – it is the mere
absence of obstructive contact.

Like unproduced space, all emptinesses are non-affirming negatives. For example, the emptiness of our body is the
mere lack, or absence, of inherent existence of our body – no
other object is implied. Thus, the mind that realizes the
emptiness of our body merely eliminates the object of negation (i.e. the inherent existence of our body) without realizing any positive phenomenon. The non-affirming negative
that is the mere absence of inherent existence of our body is
the emptiness of our body.

Both unproduced space and emptiness are non-affirming
negatives but they have different objects of negation. The
negated object of space is obstructive contact, whereas the
negated object of emptiness is inherent existence. It is
because unproduced space and emptiness differ only in
their object of negation that an understanding of unproduced space is so helpful in gaining an understanding of
emptiness.

To understand unproduced space we must first know its
negated object, obstructive contact. This is not very difficult
to know – even insects appear to know what it is. For example, an insect will walk along a table as long as it can sense
the obstructive contact of the table's surface, but it will turn

back when it reaches the edge of the table where the obstructive contact ceases. It seems that the insect knows what is obstructive contact and consequently can recognize its absence. If we ourself understand what is meant by obstructive contact, and know that unproduced space is simply the mere absence of this, we are then able to realize the meaning of unproduced space. Similarly, if we wish to realize emptiness we must first understand the negated object of emptiness, which is inherent existence. For example, in the case of the emptiness of the body, the negated object is the inherent existence of the body. In other words, the negated object is an inherently existent body. Therefore, to understand the emptiness of the body we must first be familiar with the appearance and characteristics of an inherently existent body so that we are clear which object is negated by the mind realizing emptiness.

An inherently existent body would be a body that is independent of other phenomena, including the mind apprehending it. If we check carefully we shall discover that our body appears to us to exist in this way at present. In fact, whatever appears to the mind of an ordinary being necessarily appears to be inherently existent, and for this reason all the minds of ordinary beings are mistaken. Until we realize emptiness we cling very strongly to our body with the thought 'my body, my body', and the body that appears vividly to our mind at that time is an inherently existent body. Our mistaken mind believes that this body really exists, and as a result we cling to it and develop strong attachment towards it. We then cherish this body, worry about it, and do many actions for its sake. In fact, this body does not exist at all. Thus, the body that we normally perceive and cling to as 'my body' is the actual negated object of the emptiness of our body. The body that we cling to does not exist, but we need to realize that it does not exist.

Although there does not exist anywhere an inherently existent body, the generic image of an inherently existent body does exist. A generic image is the mental image of an object that appears to our conceptual mind whenever we think about that object. For example, if we think about our mother a characteristic image of our mother appears vividly to our mind. This appearing image is the generic image of our mother. However, an object need not exist for its generic image to appear to us. For example, the generic image of a unicorn can appear vividly to our mind, but although this generic image exists, a unicorn itself does not. Similarly, whenever we think about our body, the generic image of an inherently existent body appears to our conceptual mind, but it is an image of something that is totally non-existent. Nevertheless, before we can realize correctly the emptiness of our body we must identify precisely this inherently existent body, which is the object of negation. Therefore, in meditation we need to become thoroughly familiar with the generic image of this body as it appears to us.

Buddhist philosophical treatises explain that the negated object of emptiness is inherent existence. However, if we think that we are negating inherent existence but fail to negate the body that normally appears vividly to our mind, we have not found the correct object of negation. The correct object of negation is precisely the body that we normally cling to as 'my body' and that appears to have its own existence independent of the parts of our body. Therefore, if we say that we are negating inherent existence but do not negate the body that normally appears to us, we are merely negating inherent existence 'with our mouth'.

When it is said that the body that normally appears vividly to us does not exist, some people may misunderstand this and think that the existence of phenomena is being denied completely. It is therefore very important to think deeply and with sharp wisdom about this matter. We need to identify precisely the negated object of emptiness. If the object that we negate is too extensive we shall negate something that is actually existent and thereby fall into the extreme of non-existence. This would be the case if we deny that our body exists at all. On the other hand, if the object that we negate is too limited we shall continue to accept a degree of inherent existence and thereby fall into the extreme of existence. For example, if we negate a body that is independent of its parts but posit a body that possesses its own inherent nature, there still remains an object to be negated and we have fallen into the second extreme.

The correct view of emptiness avoids both extremes and therefore emptiness is called the 'middle way'. The extreme of non-existence is avoided because the correct view of emptiness accepts the existence of phenomena that are merely imputed in dependence upon a valid basis of imputation. The extreme of existence is avoided because the correct view of emptiness thoroughly negates all traces of inherent, independent existence.

If we wish to understand emptiness clearly without any mistake and already have a basic understanding of Buddhist teachings, then upon this basis it is very important to practise purification and accumulate merit. Having prepared our mind in this way, if we then study and meditate on emptiness continually, there is great hope that we shall attain a correct realization of emptiness.

Although we need to strive to develop a new realization of emptiness it is important to understand that emptiness itself is not a new development or creation. It is not a product of philosophical analysis nor an invention of Buddha. Emptiness has been the actual nature of all phenomena from the very beginning. Our body, for example, has always been empty of inherent existence; there has never been a time when our body, or anything else, existed inherently. Although emptiness has always been the true nature of phenomena, we need to receive instructions in order to realize this; and for this reason Buddha delivered the *Perfection of Wisdom Sutras*.

It is important for us to strive to understand the emptiness of phenomena because all the problems and suffering experienced by us and other living beings stem from a mistaken view of reality. Through our ignorance of the true nature of phenomena we develop the conceptual mind that holds phenomena to be inherently existent. This mind is known as 'self-grasping' because it apprehends, or grasps, phenomena as having an inherently existent self, or identity. The mind of self-grasping gives rise to all other delusions, such as anger and attachment, and is the root cause of all suffering and dissatisfaction. Therefore if we wish to be free from suffering we must abandon our self-grasping.

To realize emptiness and overcome our self-grasping we must first receive correct instructions and then meditate on how our body and other phenomena are empty of inherent existence. First we should do analytical meditation by investigating with our wisdom whether we can find our body. Is this body that we cherish as 'my body' the same as the parts of our body? Is our head, our arms, and so forth our body? Can we find a body that is different to the parts of our body? Through this investigation we shall discover that our body is unfindable. If our analytical meditation is successful the appearance of our body will fade and there will arise an appearance of 'empty'. This emptiness is our body's emptiness of inherent existence. We should try to hold the generic image of this emptiness single-pointedly in placement meditation. If we begin to lose the generic image of emptiness we should recall the reasons used to establish our body's emptiness and thereby restore our object of meditation. Through this meditation we can become familiar with emptiness and strengthen our realization.

In the beginning during our meditations on emptiness we should not worry about falling into the extreme of non-existence because during meditation we are not performing actions of body and speech. It is when we are out of meditation and performing various actions that we need to be careful to avoid this extreme. However, if we identify correctly the negated object of emptiness there is no danger of developing extreme views. We need to know that our body does not exist inherently but does exist conventionally.

The conventional nature of our body is explained in the next chapter.

If during our meditation on emptiness we develop any doubts or see any contradictions we should discuss these afterwards with a skilled Teacher or experienced friends. In Tibet, when a Lama gave instructions on emptiness and so forth, the students would listen and then meditate on the teachings for a few days. They would then describe their experiences to the Lama and discuss any problems they were having. In this way all doubts were clarified and the students then returned to their meditation. That is the way we should try to realize emptiness. If we develop doubts or cannot accept what is taught we should discuss the matter with others. In this way our understanding will become clearer and clearer. We should not keep doubts hidden inside our hearts – we need wisdom in our hearts, not doubts!

Through receiving instructions and then contemplating and meditating on the meaning we can realize that our body and other forms are unfindable upon investigation. This unfindability is our body's emptiness of inherent existence. It indicates that our body does not exist objectively, from its own side. Our body is only a mere apprehension of the mind, a mere appearance to the mind. Perceiving this appearance we say 'my body', but if we are not satisfied with the mere name 'my body' and try to find a body existing from its own side we shall be completely unsuccessful. Through meditating on the emptiness of our body as described, our delusions such as attachment towards our body will be subdued. Similarly, if we have problems of strong attachment towards the bodies of others we can contemplate how they are also empty of inherent existence, and in this way our attachment will be reduced.

Through improving our understanding of emptiness we can build the foundation for attaining ultimate happiness. Whether we are rich or poor, beautiful or ugly, we can solve all our problems and fulfil all our wishes through the wisdom that realizes emptiness. By doing continual meditation on emptiness we shall gradually gain freedom from all suffering by uprooting its cause, ignorance. Then, even if we wish for suffering we shall be unable to experience it! If we gain the wisdom realizing emptiness we shall be like a king and our wisdom realizing emptiness will be like the king's ministers. Just as all the king's wishes are accomplished by his ministers, so too will all our wishes be accomplished by our wisdom realizing emptiness.

Although our body has been taken as the basis for establishing emptiness, all other form, and indeed all phenomena, are empty of inherent existence in the same way. To realize that all phenomena are empty of inherent existence we do not need to realize the emptiness of each phenomenon one by one. If we understand emptiness correctly using one basis such as our body, we can, without difficulty, realize the emptiness of other phenomena by changing the basis of emptiness.

In summary, Avalokiteshvara's words 'form is empty' teach that all form is empty of inherent existence – this emptiness being the first profundity of form, the profundity of the ultimate. Without realizing this profundity we cannot gain complete freedom from suffering nor full enlightenment. Thus, Avalokiteshvara indicates that the principal

practice of the perfection of wisdom while on the Mahayana paths of accumulation and preparation is meditation
on emptiness. On these two paths we need to realize emptiness inferentially using the type of reasoning described in
this chapter.

The Paths of Accumulation
and Preparation (2)

In the previous chapter an explanation was given of the first profundity of form as stated in the Sutra by the words 'form is empty'. Through this presentation of the first profundity the ultimate nature of form is revealed. The next part of Avalokiteshvara's answer presents the three remaining profundities of form and thereby reveals form's conventional nature.

THE MEDITATION ON THE SECOND PROFUNDITY OF THE AGGREGATE OF FORM

'Emptiness is form'

Whereas the first profundity of a phenomenon is the phenomenon's emptiness of inherent existence, the second profundity is the phenomenon's being a manifestation of emptiness. Because this is part of a phenomenon's conventional nature, the second profundity is called the 'profundity of the conventional'.

Although the second, third, and fourth profundities are all part of the conventional nature of phenomena, they are called 'profundities' because they are the subtle conventional nature of phenomena, which is even more difficult to realize than phenomena's ultimate nature. Furthermore, we cannot gain a perfect and complete understanding of profound emptiness until we have understood the subtle conventional nature of phenomena.

To understand what is meant by the ultimate and the conventional natures of phenomena we need to understand what is meant by the two truths – ultimate truths and conventional truths. The two truths are actual objects, or phenomena, and not just abstract philosophical laws or principles. In fact, every phenomenon that exists is either an ultimate truth or a conventional truth, but no phenomenon can be both.

Ultimate truth and emptiness of inherent existence are synonyms – whatever is an ultimate truth is an emptiness of inherent existence, and whatever is an emptiness of inherent existence is an ultimate truth. The emptiness of inherent existence of our body and the emptiness of inherent existence of this book are two examples of ultimate truths. All ultimate truths are the same in that they are emptinesses of inherent existence, but they differ in the basis of emptiness, the object that is empty.

An emptiness is called an 'ultimate truth' (Tib. dön dam denpa), literally a 'sacred object truth', because emptiness is both a sacred object and a truth. It is a sacred object because the realization of emptiness opens the door of liberation – we may realize many other phenomena but if we do not realize emptiness we shall be unable to gain liberation. An emptiness is a truth because its appearance to a non-conceptual direct perceiver is in accordance with its mode of existence. To a mind realizing an emptiness directly, only emptiness appears; inherent existence does not appear at all. Thus, when cognized directly, an emptiness does not falsely appear to be inherently existent. Because its appearance does not deceive us, an emptiness is a truth.

All phenomena except emptinesses are conventional truths. For example, our body and this book are two conventional truths. Unlike ultimate truths, which are all emptinesses, conventional truths are extremely diverse since they include every object of knowledge that is not an emptiness. Conventional truths are not actually truths in the way that ultimate truths are, because their apparent mode of existence does not accord with their actual mode of existence – conventional truths appear to be inherently existent but in reality they are empty of inherent existence. Since their appearance is deceptive, conventional truths are in fact falsities rather than truths. However, they are called 'conventional truths' because they are true with respect to the conventions of ordinary people, that is, people who have not realized emptiness directly. Conventional truths are true with respect to the view of ordinary people because although conventional truths are deceptive regarding their mode of existence, they are not deceptive regarding their function and conventional characteristics. For example, a table that is apprehended by a valid mind is a conventional truth, and we can rely upon such a table to support objects and to perform the other functions of a table. Objects that are false with respect to the minds of ordinary people, such as a table seen by someone who is hallucinating, are not conventional truths. They are non-existents and cannot be relied upon to perform the functions that they appear to possess.

The term that has been translated as conventional truth (Tib. kün dzob denpa) can also be rendered as 'truth for an obscurer'. Here, 'obscurer' refers to self-grasping – the mind that conceives phenomena to be inherently existent. Phenomena other than ultimate truths are called 'truths for an obscurer' because with respect to the mind of self-grasping they are true; they appear to be inherently existent and the mind of self-grasping holds this appearance to be true. However, it does not follow that the mind of self-grasping apprehends and establishes conventional truths. The object held by self-grasping is an inherently existent object, such as an inherently existent body, and as already explained there does not exist an inherently existent object anywhere. The object held by self-grasping is therefore a non-existent and consequently is not a conventional truth. Like ultimate truths, conventional truths are established by a valid mind; and self-grasping is not a valid mind. Thus, a conventional object is called a 'truth for an obscurer' not because the object is established by the mind of self-grasping, but because self-grasping ignorantly conceives the apparent inherent existence of the object to be true.

As we can understand from the above, it is important to distinguish between conventional truths and non-existents. A traditional example of a non-existent is a horn on the head of a rabbit. Although the ears of a rabbit can appear as a horn and we can conceive of a rabbit having a horn, we know that this appearance is mistaken and the conception is false. A horn on a rabbit's head is not established by any valid mind, and consequently it is a non-existent rather than a conventional (or ultimate) truth. In the same way, although inherently existent objects appear to the mind and are objects of conception, they are totally non-existent and therefore are not conventional truths.

Thus, when it is said that a table is a conventional truth, the meaning is that the table that is apprehended by a valid mind is a conventional truth; it does not mean that the inherently existent table that appears to the minds of ordinary beings is a conventional truth. For example, if we perceive a table with a valid eye consciousness, unless we are a fully enlightened being the table will appear to be inherently existent to our eye consciousness. However, our eye consciousness does not apprehend the table to be inherently existent; it apprehends simply the table itself. The table that is correctly apprehended by our eye consciousness in this way is a conventional truth and does exist (but not inherently). It is probable that following the valid eye consciousness that apprehends just the table itself we shall develop a conceptual mental consciousness that apprehends the table as inherently existent. This conceptual mind is a mind of self-grasping. It is a non-valid mind and the object it grasps is a non-existent.

We can now consider what is meant by the ultimate nature and the conventional nature of phenomena. The ultimate nature of a phenomenon is the phenomenon's emptiness of inherent existence, and because it is an emptiness it

is an ultimate truth. The conventional nature of a phenomenon is the phenomenon's nature as established by a valid
mind, but excluding emptiness of inherent existence. Since
the conventional nature is established by a valid mind it is
an existent; and since it is an existent and it is not an emptiness it is a conventional truth. We can consider a table as an
example to illustrate the meaning of these two natures. The
table's emptiness of inherent existence is the table's ultimate nature; the table itself and its shape, colour, and so
forth are all the conventional nature of the table. Any phenomenon such as a table has an ultimate nature and a conventional nature. The former is an ultimate truth and the
latter is a conventional truth.

The conventional nature of an object can have many
aspects. Some of these aspects can be realized simply by
direct sense awareness, such as an object's shape and colour; others are more difficult to realize, such as an object's
impermanence; and some aspects of the conventional nature
of an object can only be realized after having realized the
object's ultimate nature. That part of the conventional nature
of an object that cannot be realized without first realizing
the object's ultimate nature is the subtle conventional nature
of the object.

As already stated, the profundity of the conventional –
the second of the four profundities – is phenomena's being
a manifestation of emptiness, and is part of phenomena's
subtle conventional nature. It is part of the conventional
nature rather than the ultimate nature because it is not an
emptiness and is therefore a conventional truth rather than
an ultimate truth. It is part of the subtle conventional nature

of phenomena because we cannot realize that phenomena are a manifestation of emptiness before we realize that phenomena are empty of inherent existence.

There are many scriptural references to phenomena as the manifestation of emptiness. For example, in *Song of Emptiness* Changkya Rölpai Dorje says:

These various apprehended [objects] and apprehenders are the manifestation of the mother. This birth, death, and these changing [things] are the falsities of the mother.

Here, 'mother' refers to emptiness, and 'falsities' refers to the false appearance of conventional truths.

When Avalokiteshvara says 'emptiness is form' he is declaring the second profundity of form – that form is a manifestation of emptiness. What does it mean to say that form is a manifestation of emptiness? We have seen that the ultimate nature of our body is our body's emptiness of inherent existence. When we search for our body we can find nothing that exists from its own side; there is a complete absence, or lack, of inherent existence. Nevertheless, from its emptiness a body appears to our mind. We can say therefore that our body is a manifestation of its emptiness. This implies that our body is not separate from its emptiness but is an appearance arising out of it.

The relationship between our body and its emptiness can be illustrated by taking the example of a gold coin. The underlying nature of the coin is gold; it is the gold itself that appears in the form of a coin. Clearly, the coin that appears to us is not separate from its gold and could not exist without it. We can say therefore that the coin is a manifestation of its gold. In this analogy the gold represents the emptiness of our body and the coin represents our body itself. Just as the coin is a manifestation of its gold, our body is a manifestation of its emptiness of inherent existence.

We can consider a rather more subtle illustration of the relationship between our body and its emptiness. A sky that is completely clear appears to us as blue. We know that the actual nature of the sky is merely empty, just as the space around us is empty. Although the sky appears to be a blue canopy, if we travel towards it we shall never encounter a blue object; there is only space. Nevertheless, when we look at the sky we see blue and we point to this blue as being the sky. We can say therefore that the blue we see directly is a manifestation of an empty sky. Thus, from an empty sky, blue manifests. Similarly, from the emptiness of form, form manifests. In the same way, all phenomena are manifestations of their emptiness.

To understand the second profundity it is helpful to realize that all phenomena are a mere appearance. The use of the word 'mere' eliminates any possibility of inherent existence. Our body appears vividly to our mind, yet, as we have seen, if we search for a body existing from its own side giving rise to that appearance we cannot find such a body. How, then, does our body exist? In dependence upon a suitable basis our body is imputed by mind. The suitable basis for imputing our body is the appearance to a mind of the components of our body – our head, arms, legs, and so on. Here, appearance does not just mean appearance to eye consciousness; it includes the sounds of our body that appear to ear consciousness, the tactile sensations that appear to body consciousness when the different parts of our body are touched, and so forth. Based upon this complex pattern of appearances to consciousness our body is imputed. If we try to find a body that is more than just these appearances to consciousness we shall not succeed. Therefore, we can say that our body is a mere appearance.

All other forms exist in the same way. For example, the colour red appears vividly to our eye consciousness, but if we try to find a colour red that is more than this mere appearance we are unable to do so. If we investigate the colour red scientifically we may infer that it is a certain frequency of electromagnetic radiation, but if we investigate further we shall find that the electromagnetic radiation does not exist from its own side. It is also a mere appearance to our mind.

To illustrate how form is a mere appearance we can consider the example of a rainbow. Under certain conditions a rainbow appears in the sky. To the observer it appears as though the rainbow has a certain size, shape, and location in space. It seems to have its own existence, perhaps three or four miles away. However, we know that if we travel to the apparent location of the rainbow there will be no trace of a rainbow there at all. We can say therefore that the rainbow is a mere appearance and cannot be found upon investigation. Although other objects, such as our body, seem to have a more concrete existence, if we investigate carefully we shall discover that they too are a mere appearance.

Through our experience we know that the appearance of a rainbow is deceptive. It appears to have its own independent existence but we know that its existence depends upon the sun, the rain, and the position of the observer. If the observer moves, the rainbow moves; if the sun goes behind a cloud, the rainbow fades or disappears. Provided that we accept that the rainbow is only an appearance that arises in dependence upon certain causes and conditions, we can accept its existence and behave appropriately. However, if we cling to the idea that the rainbow exists independently of us and is fixed in space in the way that it appears, we may travel in search of the 'end of the rainbow' and experience only frustration.

The same is true of all form and of phenomena in general. If we accept them as mere appearances we can establish their existence and relate to them appropriately, without experiencing any problems. Again, though, if we cling to phenomena as existing inherently in the way that they appear we shall experience constant problems and frustration. Just as through experience we have learnt the real nature of a rainbow, so through study and contemplation we can understand the subtle conventional nature of form and other phenomena and begin to relate to them appropriately.

Another aspect of the subtle conventional nature of phenomena is that phenomena are mere name. This does not mean that the name of a phenomenon is the phenomenon itself. A name is a sound, such as the sound uttered when we say 'my body'. It is obvious that this sound is not identical with our body, since our body can sit down whereas the sound cannot! Nevertheless, if we search for the body that exists in itself as 'my body' independent of its name, we cannot find it. The parts of our body appear to our consciousness, and in dependence upon this basis we impute the name 'my body'. If this name had not been given, the phenomenon 'my body' would not exist. Without naming 'my body', the parts of our body such as 'my head' would exist provided that they had been named, but there would be no such phenomenon as 'my body'. In this sense, phenomena are mere name.

Again, an example can help us to understand this point. We can imagine a committee consisting of a number of members, one of whom is called John. Let us suppose that today John is elected to be the Chairperson of the committee. From today, John will be called the 'Chairperson' and the other committee members will think of him as the Chairperson. The John of yesterday was not the Chairperson whereas the John of today is the Chairperson, but from John's side there has been no particular change. John is now the Chairperson simply because he was so named by the committee. If we try to find something that from its own side is inherently a chairperson, we shall not succeed. John's body is not a chairperson, his mind is not a chairperson, and we shall not find anything else that is a chairperson. In this example it is not difficult to understand that 'Chairperson' is no more than name. In fact, if we investigate carefully we shall discover that all phenomena exist in this way as mere name. Indeed, in the *Perfection of Wisdom Sutra in One Hundred Thousand Lines* Buddha says 'Shariputra, know that all phenomena are mere name.'

Understanding that form is a mere appearance and mere
name helps us to understand that form is a manifestation of
emptiness. If we realize this we can establish the existence
of form without implying that form exists inherently. We
can then begin to understand the subtle conventional
nature of form and we shall be able to avoid the two
extremes of existence and non-existence.

The way in which the Madhyamika-Prasangikas establish the existence of conventional phenomena is actually in
accordance with the view of ordinary people. In establishing the existence of a table, for example, ordinary people are
content with the appearance of a table and the name 'table'.
They do not normally carry out an investigation to find the
real table. In a similar way, Madhyamika-Prasangikas say
that phenomena are merely an appearance to our mind and
mere name. They assert that if we try to find a real table
apart from the mere appearance and the mere name we
shall not succeed.

In contrast to ordinary people and to the Madhyamika-
Prasangikas, other philosophical systems, including the
lower Buddhist schools, assert that through investigation
we can discover the real object. For example, some
Buddhist schools, when they seek the table among its parts,
conclude that the mere collection of the parts of the table is
the table. They say that this collection is the real, truly existent table. According to the Madhyamika-Prasangikas this
view contradicts the view of ordinary people because the
table established in this way is not the table apprehended
by ordinary people; it is merely a fabrication of philosophical analysis. The Madhyamika-Prasangikas say that there is

no such thing as a truly existent phenomenon and so the table that the lower schools try to establish is in fact non-existent. For this reason Chandrakirti warned the lower schools not to debate with ordinary people, for if they did so they would lose!

Although the Madhyamika-Prasangikas establish the existence of conventional phenomena in accordance with the view of ordinary people, their view of the ultimate nature of phenomena contradicts the view of ordinary people. Ordinary people not only accept the existence of objects that appear to them, but they also accept objects to be inherently existent in the way that they appear. The Madhyamika-Prasangika view is that all objects are empty of inherent existence, and therefore although the existence of conventional objects is to be accepted, we must overcome the mind that grasps at inherent existence if we wish to attain liberation. Furthermore, if we wish to attain full enlightenment we must overcome even the appearance of objects as inherently existent.

Once we realize that phenomena are empty of inherent existence we can begin to understand their subtle conventional nature by meditating upon them as manifestations of emptiness using some of the reasons and examples given in this chapter. The practice of seeing phenomena as manifestations of emptiness can then be carried over into our daily activities. Although we cannot meditate on emptiness while we are eating, working, talking to others, and so forth, we can nevertheless see the objects around us as manifestations of emptiness. If we do this, our food, our body, our friends, and so forth will still appear to be inherently existent, but we shall not accept this appearance. We can continue to perform our normal functions, yet at the same time we shall implicitly be meditating on emptiness and increasing our wisdom. If we see everything as manifestations of emptiness, our mind will naturally be free from delusions and our actions will be virtuous. Through this practice our everyday activities can become extremely meaningful.

Emptiness is a permanent phenomenon, but the manifestation of emptiness need not be permanent. Functioning things such as our body are impermanent, momentary phenomena, being the result of past causes and the cause of future effects. Nevertheless all functioning things are manifestations of emptiness. Our body functions and changes moment by moment but it does not exist from its own side; it is merely imputed by thought. Our body remains empty of inherent existence at all times, and out of this permanent emptiness our body appears to us in its constantly changing form.

With respect to the minds of Superior beings, conventional truths such as our body are false. However, conventional truths are true with respect to the minds of ordinary beings because the mind of self-grasping of these beings holds the apparent inherent existence of conventional truths to be true. We need to understand that the forms and so forth that appear to us are manifestations of their emptiness and are mere name, but that they function and appear true to ordinary beings. Therefore, when performing our everyday activities we should be satisfied with the mere name of phenomena without investigating them further. At that time there is no point in trying to discover a truly existent phenomenon, because no such phenomenon can be found.

If having realized emptiness we are able to accept phenomena as mere name and engage in our various activities on this basis, this indicates that we have realized the subtle conventional nature of phenomena. Then we can still say that a particular object is large or small, for example, but we know that the object is mere name and cannot be found upon analysis.

If we have this correct understanding of the subtle conventional nature of phenomena, we can understand that phenomena are empty of inherent existence but also perform their individual functions. In this way the conventional nature of phenomena and their emptiness of inherent existence are seen not as contradictory but as mutually supportive. For example, realizing the emptiness of inherent existence of our body helps us to understand the conventional nature of our body as mere name or mere appearance, and realizing that our body is mere name helps us to understand that our body is empty of inherent existence. We need to strive to realize the two truths in this way.

THE MEDITATION ON THE THIRD PROFUNDITY OF
THE AGGREGATE OF FORM

'Emptiness is not other than form; form also is not other than emptiness.'

In this next part of his answer Avalokiteshvara continues to explain the conventional nature of form by revealing the third profundity. The third profundity is the profundity of

Maitreya

the two truths being the same entity, and, like the second profundity, it is part of the subtle conventional nature of phenomena. If we realize the third profundity we realize that the conventional nature and the ultimate nature of a phenomenon are the same entity. The third profundity does not imply that the two truths are identical, but rather that they do not exist as separate entities.

If, like the two truths, two phenomena are the same entity but not identical, they do not appear as separate to a non-conceptual direct perceiver, but they appear as different to a conceptual mind. If two phenomena are identical they have the same generic image. This can be better understood by considering examples.

The shape of our body and our body itself are an example of two phenomena that are not identical but are the same entity. Quite clearly, the shape of our body cannot appear to a non-conceptual direct perceiver as separate from our body itself. This indicates that the two are the same entity. Nevertheless, we would not say that our body and its shape are identical phenomena, because they appear as different to our conception. For example, we conceive of our body as a phenomenon having a certain weight, colour, smell, and so forth, whereas the shape of our body does not have these characteristics. Another example of two phenomena that are not identical but are the same entity is a fire and the heat of the fire. Although these two can be distinguished, they never appear to a non-conceptual direct perceiver as being separate.

By contrast, if we consider this book and our body, these two phenomena appear as quite separate to a non-conceptual direct perceiver; the book appears in one place and our body in another. This indicates that the book and our body are two phenomena that are different entities.

The meaning of Avalokiteshvara's statement, 'Emptiness is not other than form; form also is not other than emptiness', is that form is the same entity as the emptiness of form. It therefore reveals the third profundity of form. The emptiness referred to in Avalokiteshvara's statement is specifically the emptiness of form; form is not the same entity as emptiness in general. For example, form is not the same entity as the emptiness of feeling; form and the emptiness of feeling exist separately. Thus, when it is said that the two truths are the same entity, it does not mean that all ultimate truths are the same entity as all conventional truths, but rather that the ultimate nature and conventional nature of a particular phenomenon, such as our body, are the same entity.

When we look at our body, our body and the shape of our body appear simultaneously to our direct eye awareness. We never develop the thought that our body and its shape are separate entities. However, unless we have attained full enlightenment, our body and our body's emptiness of inherent existence do not appear simultaneously to our non-conceptual mind. This is because we have strong imprints of conceiving our body and its emptiness to be completely different entities. For countless lifetimes we have conceived phenomena to be inherently existent. As a result of this conception and its imprints, phenomena appear to us to be inherently existent. When we directly perceive a form, such as our body, not only does the form appear to us, but also the form's inherent existence appears. Therefore, for ordinary beings, form and the inherent existence of form (rather than the emptiness of inherent existence of form) seem to be the same entity!

When emptiness is explained to us, the two truths appear to be two distinct and separate phenomena, like a table and a chair. Having first realized emptiness the two truths still do not appear directly and simultaneously to our mind. This is because we still have a mind that holds the two truths to be different entities. Even high Bodhisattvas who have overcome all delusions have the imprints of that mind, and therefore even these Bodhisattvas cannot directly realize the two truths simultaneously. Consequently, they cannot maintain meditative equipoise on emptiness while performing other actions of body, speech, and mind. When they engage in bodily and verbal actions Bodhisattvas must temporarily relinquish the mind that directly realizes emptiness, and when they wish to engage in meditative equipoise on emptiness they must disengage from other actions. Only Buddhas have completely overcome both the mind that apprehends the two truths as different entities and the imprints of this mind. Because they are completely free from this mind and its imprints, Buddhas are able to realize the two truths directly and simultaneously. Therefore they are able to perform any action of body, speech, and mind while maintaining their meditative equipoise on emptiness.

How can we know that the two truths are the same entity? First we must understand that phenomena are empty of inherent existence. As already mentioned, until we attain enlightenment form appears to us as inherently existent. If form really were inherently existent as it appears to us, form and the emptiness of form would not be the same entity. Therefore, before we can realize the third profundity of form we must know that what appears to us is false. At present this is difficult for us to know because it is very profound, but nevertheless we can understand it through careful investigation.

Something is true if the way it appears to us corresponds to the way it actually exists. Conversely, if something does not exist in the way that it appears, it is false. For example, we say that a mirage is a false object because it appears to be water but does not exist as water. If we investigate thoroughly we shall discover that the way our body appears also does not correspond to the way it exists – our body appears to be inherently existent but it does not exist inherently. Therefore our body is false. In the same way, all conventional truths are false and deceive us. Our body appears to us to be true and then, grasping it to be true, we develop delusions such as attachment. As a result of such delusions we perform non-virtuous actions and these cause us to experience suffering both now and in the future. This is how our body and other forms deceive us. We have cherished the independent body that appears to our mind since we were born, but if we realize emptiness we shall know that we have been making a terrible mistake. We shall know, based on the reasons already described, that this body definitely does not exist.

We can compare ourself to someone who wishes to travel to London but who has set off on the wrong road. Imagine that after travelling many miles this person meets another traveller who points out to him that he is on the wrong road and explains which is the correct road to London. The person will realize immediately that he has made a serious mistake and has been travelling in the wrong direction since setting out. He will then turn back and hopefully will follow the correct road to London. In a similar way, before realizing emptiness we are following incorrect paths. We are seeking happiness but we are following paths that lead to suffering, guided by the mind that grasps at true existence. At present we believe that whatever appears to our mind is truly existent and then we follow the paths of cyclic existence. However, once we realize emptiness through meeting correct instructions we shall know that hitherto we have been completely misled and mistaken. We shall realize that what appeared to us, what we apprehended, and the attitudes we developed were all completely wrong. Then, hopefully, we shall begin to follow the path to liberation, the path that really does lead to peace and happiness.

We can understand that the present appearance of form is false by realizing that form is empty of inherent existence. We shall then understand that emptiness of inherent existence is an inseparable characteristic of form. Realizing this, we can begin to understand that form and the emptiness of form are the same entity. For example, if the emptiness of our body is an inseparable characteristic of our body, it follows that our body and its emptiness are the same entity, just as other characteristics of our body, such as its shape, are the same entity as our body. Just as the shape of our body cannot exist separately from our body, and our body cannot exist separately from its shape, so, too, the emptiness of our body cannot exist separately from our body, and our body cannot exist separately from its emptiness.

An understanding of the second profundity of form can also help us to understand the third profundity. The second profundity of form is that form is the manifestation of the emptiness of form. If one phenomenon is the manifestation of another, the two phenomena cannot be different entities. The examples were given earlier of a coin being a manifestation of the gold from which it is made, and the colour blue being a manifestation of an empty sky. Clearly the coin does not exist as a different entity to its gold, and neither does the blue of the sky exist as a different entity to the empty sky. Likewise, if we know that form is a manifestation of the emptiness of form we can know that form and the emptiness of form are the same entity.

The emptiness of form is form's lack of inherent existence. If we ask 'What is it that lacks the inherent existence of form?', the answer is 'Form itself.' There is no emptiness of form that is separate from form, and there is no form that is separate from the emptiness of form. Therefore, form and the emptiness of form are the same entity. This is the meaning of 'Emptiness is not other than form; form also is not other than emptiness.'

Through his great skill, Buddha not only gave instructions on how to gain an initial realization of emptiness but also gave instructions on how to improve that realization. Meditation on the first profundity is the method to gain a realization of emptiness, and meditation on the last three profundities is the method to improve our meditation on emptiness, thereby making our meditation more powerful.

If we have realized that the two truths are the same entity, when we meditate on emptiness conventional phenomena will gather and absorb into emptiness like a rainbow dissolving into the sky. Through this experience we can build the foundation of our Truth Body, the Dharmakaya. The actual Truth Body is the mind of a Buddha and is the resultant perfection of wisdom. It is our ultimate object of attainment, but we cannot attain it immediately. We must first build a small foundation, improve it, and then finally we can attain the actual Truth Body of a Buddha. The Truth Body is known as the 'Great Mother of all the Buddhas' because from the Truth Body all other bodies of a Buddha arise. Thus, the Truth Body is the real body of a Buddha.

When our mind mixes permanently with emptiness, like water poured into water, this mixture is the actual Truth Body. Before we can attain this actual Truth Body we need to train in the understanding of emptiness. We must improve our meditation on emptiness by bringing our mind and its object, emptiness, closer together. The main obstacle to mixing our mind with emptiness is the appearance of conventional objects during our emptiness meditation. Whenever conventional objects appear to our mind they appear to be inherently existent, and thus their appearance during our meditation on emptiness acts as an obstacle to our perceiving emptiness directly. Therefore, before we can thoroughly mix our mind and emptiness together we need to prevent the appearance of conventional objects during our emptiness meditation.

A profound method for overcoming the appearance of conventional objects during our meditation on emptiness is to meditate on the two truths being the same entity. If we do this we shall find it easier to dissolve all appearances into emptiness. Therefore, sometimes we should meditate on emptiness, and sometimes we should meditate on the two truths being the same entity. Eventually we can overcome completely the unwanted appearance of conventional objects during our meditation on emptiness. We shall then gain a direct realization of emptiness, enabling our mind to mix with emptiness like water poured into water.

If we realize that the two truths are the same entity, all conventional objects will become equalized in the state of emptiness; we shall understand that all conventional objects are equal in the sense that they are manifestations of emptiness and are the same entity as emptiness. Before realizing this we tend to have a very unbalanced view of conventional objects; some appear to be inherently attractive and others inherently repellent. As a result we develop attachment towards some and anger or hatred towards others. Even with regard to a single object we sometimes have strong anger and sometimes strong desire. This leads to a discontented, agitated mind, and as a result we create many negative actions, causing us to experience continual problems. If we meditate on the two truths being the same entity, all objects become equalized in the state of emptiness and our unbalanced attitude decreases.

THE MEDITATION ON THE FOURTH PROFUNDITY OF
THE AGGREGATE OF FORM

The fourth profundity is the profundity of the two truths being nominally distinct. Although the two truths are the same entity they are not identical. If we understand clearly the distinction between the two truths while accepting that they are the same entity, we understand the fourth profundity.

In the *Essence of Wisdom Sutra* there is no explicit expression of the fourth profundity of form, but it is implied in the statement of the third profundity: 'Emptiness is not other than form; form also is not other than emptiness.' Explicitly this states that form and the emptiness of form are the same entity, but it also implies that the two can be distinguished. If we wish to realize the fourth profundity of form we must understand both the ultimate nature and the conventional nature of form and be able to distinguish between them. The ultimate nature of form is form's emptiness of inherent existence and has already been discussed. We can now consider the conventional nature of form in more detail.

Whereas the ultimate nature of form is a subtle phenomenon, the conventional nature of form has many aspects ranging from gross to subtle. We can consider a table as an example. The most gross conventional nature of a table includes the table's shape, colour, and so forth. We can realize this level of the conventional nature of a table directly with our sense consciousness, enabling us to distinguish a table from non-tables and this table from that table. However, if we understand only the very gross conventional nature of a table it is difficult for us to distinguish the table that is a conventional truth from the inherently existent table that is conceived by self-grasping. To make this distinction we need to realize more subtle aspects of the table's conventional nature. So it is with form in general; until we can distinguish form that is a conventional truth from inherently existent form we do not have a complete understanding of form's conventional nature.

If form were inherently existent it would be independent of all other phenomena. In fact, when we investigate we find that form exists in dependence upon other phenomena. It follows that form is not inherently existent but is a dependent-related phenomenon. Since being dependent-related is the antithesis of being inherently existent, if we can identify form that is dependent-related we can distinguish form that is a conventional truth from inherently existent form that is conceived by self-grasping. Therefore, if we wish to gain a perfect understanding of the conventional nature of form we must recognize form as a dependent-related phenomenon.

There are various ways in which form exists in a dependent relationship with other phenomena. Some types of dependence are quite gross and are comparatively easy to understand, whereas other types of dependence are subtle and more difficult to understand. There are five main ways in which form is a dependent-related phenomenon:

(1) A dependent-related phenomenon depending on causes

(2) A dependent-related phenomenon depending on name

(3) A dependent-related phenomenon depending on parts

(4) A dependent-related phenomenon depending on a basis of imputation

(5) A dependent-related phenomenon depending on mere imputation by conception

Not only form, but all impermanent phenomena are dependent-related in these five ways. Permanent phenomena, such as space and emptiness, do not arise in dependence upon causes, but are dependent-related in the last four ways.

1 A dependent-related phenomenon depending on causes. All impermanent phenomena are produced in dependence upon causes. It may be difficult in some cases to identify the cause that produced a particular phenomenon, and it may also be difficult to predict what effect will be produced by a particular collection of causes, but it is not very difficult to understand that in general all impermanent phenomena arise from appropriate causes. Before a new phenomenon can be produced, its causes must assemble. We can take the example of a sprout of wheat growing in a field. This sprout could not be produced unless its causes, such as a wheat seed, soil, and moisture, were assembled. Even after a new phenomenon, such as a sprout of wheat, has been produced, it continues to undergo change. The sprout of wheat gradually grows and eventually produces its crop of grain. We can see these gross changes taking place over a period of time, but we also know that on the atomic level countless subtle changes take place in the sprout every moment. All these changes, both gross and subtle, take place in dependence upon causes and conditions. The immediate cause of the sprout as it exists at a particular moment is the sprout as it existed in the previous moment, together with the surrounding conditions of moisture and so forth. Through the coming together of the sprout of the previous moment, soil, and moisture, the sprout of the next moment is produced. If we investigate carefully we shall understand that all changes in phenomena, however subtle, take place as a result of causes in this way.

Since each momentary state of a phenomenon arises from causes that exist in the previous moment it follows that we can trace back the causes of a phenomenon from moment to previous moment in a chain of cause and effect without beginning. There is no starting point to this process because the causes of each moment of an impermanent phenomenon are themselves impermanent phenomena and therefore have their own causes. We can take our body as an example. Our body as it exists today was produced from our body of yesterday and from the food we ate, the air we breathed, and so forth. Our body of yesterday was similarly produced from our body of the day before, and so on. Eventually we can trace back the causes of our present body to the sperm and ovum of our parents. These cells can also be traced back to previous causes in a process without beginning.

A sprout of wheat and our body are both examples of the aggregate of form. Like these two examples, all forms are impermanent – undergoing momentary change in dependence upon causes in the way that has been described. Therefore all forms exist at a particular moment in dependence upon causes, and are thus dependent-related phenomena depending on causes.

2 A dependent-related phenomenon depending on name.

As quoted earlier, Buddha says in the *Perfection of Wisdom Sutra in One Hundred Thousand Lines*: 'Shariputra, know that all phenomena are mere name.' This has already been illustrated by the example of a person called John being elected as the Chairperson of a committee. In this example it is clear that the Chairperson is no more than a name or label given to John. A chairperson comes into existence in complete dependence upon the process of naming. The same is true of forms and all other phenomena. Thus our body, a table, the colour blue, and so forth all exist in dependence upon their name.

A doubt may arise that although 'my body' is a mere name, or label, there exists an object that performs the functions of my body, and this object is more than just mere name. We may have the thought that there is an object existing in its own right that is 'waiting', as it were, to be called 'my body'. However, if we examine the basis of the name 'my body' we find that it is merely an assembly of various parts – legs, arms, a head, and so forth. We cannot find a single, discrete object that is, in itself, fit to be called 'my body'. Furthermore, if we investigate the parts of our body such as our legs we find that they too are mere name. 'Leg' is merely a name given to a certain assembly of flesh and bones. Even 'flesh' itself is no more than a name given to a collection of certain cells. We can proceed like this down to the smallest particle and we shall discover upon careful investigation that all forms and all other phenomena exist through being named. If we understand this, we realize that form is a dependent-related phenomenon depending on name.

3 A dependent-related phenomenon depending on parts. All forms have parts. Taking our body as an example, it is clear that our body is composed of many parts. As already discussed, our body is not identical with its parts, nor is it independent of its parts. If our body were identical with its parts, such as our head and our arms, we would have many bodies, since there are many parts of our body. On the other hand, if our body were independent of its parts we could remove all the parts of our body and our body itself would still remain. We must conclude that our body is different from its parts but is dependent upon them. This is true of all form, and therefore form is a dependent-related phenomenon depending on parts.

4 A dependent-related phenomenon depending on a basis of imputation. We say that we see our body when we see the parts of our body – our legs, arms, and so forth. Similarly, other people develop the thought that they are seeing or touching our body when they see or touch parts of our body. Other than the parts of our body, we have no body to be seen or touched. Clearly, the parts of our body act as the basis for designating, or imputing, our body. Our body is merely imputed, and the basis of imputation of our body is the parts of our body. By convention it is quite correct to impute 'my body' on the basis of our head, arms, and so forth, and therefore the parts of our body are the valid basis of imputation of our body. However, sometimes we impute a phenomenon upon an invalid basis, as in the example of mistaking a toy rubber snake for a real snake. In this case the basis of imputation, a length of striped rubber, is not a valid basis for imputing a snake, and therefore the snake that is imputed upon this basis does not actually exist. A phenomenon exists only if it is imputed upon a valid basis, and so no phenomenon exists without a basis of imputation. Thus form is a dependent-related phenomenon depending on a basis of imputation.

5 A dependent-related phenomenon depending on mere imputation by conception. As explained above, form depends on a valid basis of imputation. It follows that form must also depend on imputation by consciousness. For example, our body depends on its parts as a basis of imputation, but it also depends on the mind that imputes our body. These two, a valid basis of imputation and an imputing consciousness, need to come together in order to establish the existence of a phenomenon.

The mind that imputes, or designates, an object, is a conceptual mind. The first way in which a conceptual mind imputes an object is the process of naming; it is a conceptual mind that first imputes a name to a particular basis of imputation. The second way in which a conceptual mind imputes an object is by subsequently apprehending the appearance of the basis of imputation as the designated object.

We can consider again the example of John being elected as the Chairperson of his committee. The conceptual minds that originally designate John as the 'Chairperson' impute 'Chairperson' in the first manner. Through this process of naming, a new phenomenon, 'Chairperson', comes into existence. Subsequently, any conceptual mind that apprehends John as the 'Chairperson' imputes 'Chairperson' in the second manner. In the case of the Chairperson it is not difficult to understand that the phenomenon is imputed by conception. Through careful investigation we can realize that forms and all other phenomena are also imputed by conception in this way.

Form is dependent on *mere* imputation by conception because apart from the imputation by conception there is no form to be found at all. Again, considering the example of the Chairperson can help us to understand this. Clearly, if no conceptual mind designates John as the Chairperson, there is no chairperson anywhere. If we examine John's aggregates in search of a chairperson, or an indication of a chairperson, we shall find no such thing. Apart from the mere imputation by conception there is no chairperson at all. Although it is perhaps more difficult to realize, the same is true of forms such as our body, and of all other phenomena. Thus form is a dependent-related phenomenon depending on mere imputation by conception.

The five ways in which form is dependent upon other phenomena have been described in order of increasing subtlety. It is not difficult to realize that form is a dependent-related phenomenon depending on causes – the least subtle type of dependence; whereas it is very difficult to realize that form is a dependent-related phenomenon depending on mere imputation by conception – the most subtle type of dependence.

The fact that a phenomenon is dependent-related can be used as a reason for establishing the emptiness of the phenomenon. For example, if we realize that our body is a dependent-related phenomenon depending on causes, this can lead to the inferential realization that our body is empty of inherent existence. If our body were inherently existent it would have its own existence independent of all other phenomena and therefore would not depend on causes for its existence. The fact that our body does depend on causes is a clear indication that our body is not inherently existent. Similarly, our body being dependent upon name, parts, and a basis of imputation can also be used as reasons to establish an inferential realization of our body's emptiness of inherent existence.

The fifth type of dependence – dependence on mere imputation by conception – is the subtle conventional nature of phenomena and therefore cannot be realized before realizing emptiness. Since a reason used in the establishment of an inferential cognizer must already be realized before the inferential cognizer can be generated, it follows that in practice the fifth type of dependence cannot be the reason used to gain an initial realization of emptiness.

The first type of dependence is the easiest to realize and therefore can be used first as a reason for establishing emptiness. If our wisdom increases we can realize the more subtle types of dependence, and then these too can be used to establish emptiness. Although the first four types of dependence can all be used as reasons in establishing

Samantabhadra

emptiness, the more subtle the dependence, the more powerful it is as a reason.

There are many logical reasons that can be used to establish the emptiness of inherent existence of phenomena, but many texts have praised dependent relationship as 'the king of logical reasons' because of its special power. It is such a powerful reason because being dependent-related is the direct opposite of being inherently existent. Ordinary beings conceive each phenomenon to have its own existence within itself, quite separate from, and independent of, other phenomena. A realization that phenomena in fact exist in dependence upon other phenomena directly undermines this false conception of inherent existence.

When we realize that form is dependent-related to other phenomena in the five ways described, we gain a thorough understanding of the conventional nature of form. We shall then be able to distinguish the conventional nature of form from the inherently existent nature that is conceived by self-grasping. Having realized both the conventional nature and the ultimate nature of form, we shall be able to distinguish clearly between the two yet realize that they are the same entity. When we have gained this understanding we have realized the fourth profundity of form.

With the realization of just the first profundity, without having realized the other profundities, the two truths may appear to be contradictory. In this case, when we contemplate the conventional nature of a phenomenon it is difficult to accept that the phenomenon is empty of inherent existence, and when we contemplate the phenomenon's emptiness it is difficult to establish its conventional nature. However, when we gain a thorough understanding of the four profundities we shall realize that the two truths are mutually supporting. Then, when we recognize conventional truths as dependent-related our realization of emptiness is strengthened, and when we recall emptiness our recognition of conventional truths as dependent-related is reinforced. If we realize all four profundities we shall understand that form appears to our mind *because* form is empty of inherent existence, not *in spite of* its emptiness.

THE MEDITATION ON THE FOUR PROFUNDITIES OF THE AGGREGATES OF FEELING AND SO FORTH

'Likewise, feeling, discrimination, compositional factors, and consciousness are empty.'

Having revealed the four profundities of the aggregate of form, Avalokiteshvara now explains that the four profundities apply in the same way to the remaining aggregates of feeling, discrimination, compositional factors, and consciousness. This is the meaning of the next section of the Sutra quoted above.

The first profundity of feeling is feeling's emptiness of inherent existence. If we are an ordinary being, when we develop a pleasant feeling we conceive that feeling to have its own existence within itself. As a result we develop strong attachment to pleasant feelings and become upset when we cannot attain them or when they fade. Similarly, when we develop an unpleasant feeling, the feeling seems to be inherently unpleasant and existing from its own side.

However, if we investigate carefully we discover that feelings are not inherently existent in the way that we conceive them to be.

If feelings were inherently existent they would exist independently of all other phenomena. In fact, we know that feelings arise in dependence upon other phenomena. For example, if someone caresses our body gently we may develop a pleasant feeling, whereas if a person hits us sharply we develop an unpleasant feeling. In these examples it is clear that feelings are impermanent and arise in dependence upon causes. From this we can know that feelings are not inherently existent.

The remaining profundities of feeling can be established in the same way as those of form: feeling is a manifestation of the emptiness of feeling; feeling and the emptiness of feeling are the same entity; feeling and the emptiness of feeling are nominally distinct.

The four profundities also apply to the remaining aggregates of discrimination, compositional factors, and consciousness. Through the type of reasoning already described we can gain an inferential understanding of both the ultimate nature and the conventional nature of all five aggregates. Meditating on the two truths in this way, with the motivation of bodhichitta, is the method of practising the perfection of wisdom while on the Mahayana paths of accumulation and preparation.

Although in the Sutra Avalokiteshvara explicitly explains the two truths on the basis of the five aggregates, his answer also implicitly explains the two truths of persons because a person comprises five aggregates. Broadly, a person's body is the aggregate of form, and a person's mind can be divided into the remaining aggregates of feeling, discrimination, compositional factors, and consciousness. Because persons comprise their five aggregates, if we understand the four profundities of the five aggregates it is not difficult to understand the four profundities of persons.

Persons, or beings, can be considered in two categories: ourself and other beings. Other beings include all other humans, all animals, and any other beings who possess mind. Although the four profundities apply to both oneself and others in just the same way, the implications are more powerful when we apply them to ourself.

Until we have realized the emptiness of persons we conceive ourself to be inherently existent. We conceive of a me or I that has its own independent existence. The I that we grasp is neither our body nor our mind but appears to be a self-existent entity existing independently of our body and mind. The meaning of an inherently existent I is an I that exists from its own side without depending on other phenomena. If we check carefully, we shall realize that this is precisely how we consider ourself to exist at present.

If there were an inherently existent I, it could be mentally or physically separated from other phenomena because it would not depend upon them. Therefore if our I really is inherently existent we must be able to find it through analysis. We can carry out an investigation to see whether we can in fact find our I, just as we tried earlier to find our body.

Our I must be either the same as our five aggregates or different from them – there is no other possibility. We can check first whether we can find an I that is the same as our five aggregates. When we consider our aggregates, five different phenomena appear to our mind – the aggregates of form, feeling, discrimination, compositional factors, and consciousness. If our I is identical with our five aggregates, then when we consider our I, five different phenomena should also appear to our mind. But there is no one who considers his or her I to be fivefold in this way. The I that we cling to is definitely single, and therefore we can conclude that it is not identical with the five aggregates. Also, the fact that we talk of 'my body' and 'my mind' indicates that we consider our I to be the possessor of our physical and mental aggregates rather than to be the aggregates themselves.

We can now check whether we can find an I that is different to the five aggregates. If our I can be found upon analysis and it is different to our aggregates, then we can remove our aggregates and our I will remain. However, if we do remove our physical and mental aggregates there is no part of us remaining – there is definitely no I existing separately from our aggregates. Also, if we check carefully we shall realize that we cannot be perceived without our aggregates being perceived. This indicates that our I does not exist separately from our aggregates.

By carrying out this type of analysis we can satisfy ourself that there is nothing we can point to and identify as our I – our aggregates are not our I, and there is no I to be found that is different from our aggregates. The conclusion must be that there is no I that can be found upon analysis and thus there is no inherently existent I. It follows that the very concrete I that appears vividly to our mind and that seems to be in charge of our mind and body is only a mental fabrication and has no existence in reality. If through meditation we realize this, the strong appearance of an inherently existent I will fade and we shall perceive an emptiness in its place. If we have carried out a correct analysis, the emptiness that appears to our mind at that time is the emptiness of inherent existence of our self. We can apply the same arguments to realize the emptiness of inherent existence of other persons and thereby realize the first profundity of persons.

Having realized the first profundity of persons, the second and third profundities follow as they did in the case of the five aggregates. Like the aggregates, persons are a manifestation of emptiness – this is the second profundity of persons. Also, there is no person who is separate from the emptiness of the person. Realizing this, we can understand the third profundity of persons, which is that a person and the emptiness of the person are the same entity. The fourth profundity of persons is the nominal distinction between the conventional nature and the ultimate nature of persons. To gain a proper understanding of the conventional nature of persons it is necessary to recognize persons as dependent-related phenomena. As in the case of the five aggregates, persons are dependent-related phenomena on five levels.

1 A dependent-related phenomenon depending on causes. It is not difficult to realize that we and all other beings arise in dependence upon causes. To begin with, our birth as a human being quite clearly depended on our parents and many other conditions. Since then we have undergone countless changes, and all these changes have occurred as a result of various causes and conditions. The way we exist at any particular moment is therefore the result of a chain of cause and effect with no beginning. By considering this we can understand that a person is a dependent-related phenomenon depending on causes.

2 A dependent-related phenomenon depending on name. The example has already been given of a person called John being elected as the Chairperson of a committee. It is quite clear that the phenomenon 'Chairperson' is no more than a name given to John. There is no chairperson existing in himself as a chairperson. We may feel that although this is true of 'Chairperson', John himself is more than mere name. However, if we consider the matter carefully we can understand that John exists in the same way as the Chairperson. 'John' is merely a name given to a particular collection of aggregates, and thus John comes into existence through being named. We might argue that before John is named there exists a person, whatever we choose to call him, and that this person exists independently of any name. But again if we check carefully we shall discover that to call the collection of a mind and body a 'person' is also a process of naming and is not fundamentally different to calling such a collection the 'Chairperson'. Even 'me' or 'I' are merely names given to the collection of our aggregates – we cannot find a me that exists independently of this name. It follows that a person, like all other phenomena, is a dependent-related phenomenon depending on name.

3 A dependent-related phenomenon depending on parts.
A person, like other objects, has many parts. We can consider a person as consisting of the five aggregates already discussed, and each of these aggregates can be further divided. If the various parts of a person's body and mind were removed there would be no person remaining at all. This indicates that a person is a dependent-related phenomenon depending on parts.

4 A dependent-related phenomenon depending on a basis of imputation. As already discussed, a person exists in dependence upon name. However, a name alone is not sufficient to establish the existence of a person. We cannot point to an empty space and validly call it 'Peter'! To establish the existence of a person there must be a valid basis of designation, or imputation, of that person. The valid basis of imputation of a person is the person's five aggregates. Thus, when we see Peter's form aggregate we say that we are seeing Peter. In this example, Peter's form aggregate acts as the principal basis for imputing Peter. Similarly, if we are experiencing an unpleasant feeling we say that we are unhappy. In this case our aggregate of feeling acts as the principal basis for imputing me. As already explained, the five aggregates of a person are not the person but they act as the basis upon which the person is imputed. Without this basis there is no person. It follows that a person is a dependent-related phenomenon depending on a basis of imputation.

5 A dependent-related phenomenon depending on mere imputation by conception. It has been shown that a person depends on name and on a basis of imputation. However, these two alone do not establish the existence of a person. There must also be a conceptual mind that imputes the name upon the basis of imputation. For example, a person called 'Peter' comes into existence through a conceptual mind giving this name to a collection of five aggregates. Subsequently other conceptual minds will apprehend this person's five aggregates as Peter. Similarly our conceptual mind imputes me or I upon our five aggregates. If we try to find a me that is more than this mere imputation by conception we shall not succeed. Therefore a person is a dependent-related phenomenon depending on mere imputation by conception.

By realizing that we, as a person, are a dependent-related phenomenon in the five ways described, we can clearly identify the I that is a conventional truth and distinguish it from the inherently existent I that appears to our mind yet does not exist. If we correctly recognize the conventional nature of ourself and other persons in this way, as well as realizing that persons are empty of inherent existence we shall have a proper understanding of the fourth profundity with regard to persons.

Through realizing the four profundities of persons we can understand both the ultimate and conventional nature of ourself and others. This understanding is essential if we wish to overcome our delusions, the source of our suffering, because most of our deluded states of mind are rooted in the belief that there is an inherently existent me or self. Through this belief we generate the mind that strongly wishes to protect and cherish this self, which then leads us to develop anger, attachment, jealousy, pride, and so forth. These delusions destroy our peace of mind and cause us to create actions that perpetuate our dissatisfaction and suffering. In fact, if we investigate carefully we shall realize that all our unhappiness is caused by our mind of self-cherishing, which in turn is based on grasping at an inherently existent self. It is therefore very important that we gain a proper understanding of the four profundities of persons.

The part of Avalokiteshvara's answer revealing the four profundities of the five aggregates, and, indirectly, of persons, has now been discussed. This section of the Sutra provides an extensive explanation of how to practise the perfection of wisdom on the Mahayana paths of accumulation and preparation. On these paths we need to gain an inferential realization of the two truths in dependence upon correct reasoning in the way described.

The Path of Seeing

'Shariputra, like this all phenomena are merely empty,
having no characteristics. They are not produced and
do not cease. They have no defilement and no separation from defilement. They have no decrease and no
increase.'

In this part of his answer Avalokiteshvara explains how we
should practise the perfection of wisdom while on the
Mahayana path of seeing, the third Mahayana path. The
meaning of his answer will be explained after a brief
description of the way in which a Bodhisattva attains the
path of seeing.

On the paths of accumulation and preparation we realize
emptiness with a conceptual mind by relying upon correct
reasons that we have previously established firmly in our
mind. When we first realize emptiness in this way, we have

the experience that our mind and emptiness are quite separate. Our mind appears to be on one side and its object, emptiness, appears to be on the other side; the two are not mixed. Although such a realization of emptiness is a profound attainment, it does not have the power to overcome our delusions completely. Before we can completely overcome our delusions we need to gain a direct realization of emptiness with a non-conceptual mind that is able to mix with emptiness like water poured into water. To gain a direct realization of emptiness we need gradually to close the gap between our mind and emptiness by overcoming dualistic appearance during our meditation.

Whenever a conventional object appears to the mind of a sentient being, not only does the object itself appear to the mind, but also the inherent existence of the object appears simultaneously. The appearance to a mind of an object together with the appearance to that mind of the object's inherent existence is known as 'dualistic appearance'. Any mind that has dualistic appearance is a mistaken awareness because its object mistakenly appears to be inherently existent. All minds of sentient beings except the exalted awareness of meditative equipoise of a Superior being are mistaken awarenesses because all these minds have dualistic appearance.

Dualistic appearance is the principal obstacle to realizing emptiness directly. If a mind experiences dualistic appearance, inherent existence appears to that mind, and this appearance prevents the direct perception of emptiness. To prevent dualistic appearance during our meditation on emptiness, we must overcome the appearance of all conventional objects during our meditation, so that the only object we perceive at that time is profound emptiness.

Since the mind that realizes emptiness while we are on the paths of accumulation and preparation is a conceptual mind, the appearance of emptiness to that mind is mixed with the appearance of the generic image of emptiness. Although emptiness itself is an ultimate truth, the generic image of emptiness is a conventional truth. Therefore, to prevent dualistic appearance during our meditation on emptiness we must eventually overcome the appearance of the generic image of emptiness and thereby perceive emptiness directly.

When we first realize emptiness conceptually we still have gross dualistic appearance during our meditation on emptiness; there is still the strong appearance of conventional objects, and consequently there is a large gap between our mind and emptiness. If we continue to meditate on emptiness and improve our realization, the appearance of conventional objects becomes weaker during our meditation on emptiness. In this way the dualistic appearance becomes more subtle and the gap that we experience between our mind and its object, emptiness, becomes smaller. As we progress towards the end of the path of preparation, the appearance of the generic image of emptiness fades and the appearance of emptiness itself becomes stronger. Eventually the appearance of the generic image of emptiness ceases completely and we realize emptiness directly with a non-conceptual mind that is free from dualistic appearance. When we develop this mind we have no experience of our mind and emptiness being separate;

they appear to be mixed together and indistinguishable, like water poured into water. The moment that we realize emptiness directly in this way we have entered the path of seeing and have become a Superior being. At that moment also we have become a Sangha Jewel and thus an object of refuge. The direct realization of emptiness on the path of seeing is much more powerful than the conceptual realization of emptiness on the previous paths. With this direct realization of emptiness we can begin to overcome the seeds of delusions.

When we first realize emptiness directly we attain the uninterrupted path of the path of seeing. It is called an 'uninterrupted path' because on this path we abandon without interruption all our intellectually-formed delusions and their seeds. An intellectually-formed delusion is a delusion that has developed as a result of mistaken philosophical beliefs. For example, if we adhere to a philosophy that propounds the existence of an eternal, unchanging soul or self, the mind of self-grasping that results from this belief is an intellectually-formed delusion. The uninterrupted path of the path of seeing is an exalted awareness of meditative equipoise that is the direct antidote to intellectually-formed delusions, and these are abandoned during a single meditative equipoise. While remaining in that same meditative equipoise, the moment that we have abandoned our intellectually-formed delusions we have progressed to the released path of the path of seeing. It is called a 'released path' because on this path we have been released from the delusions that we abandoned during the previous uninterrupted path. When we arise from the single meditative equipoise that comprises the uninterrupted path and the released path of the path of seeing, we are still on the path of seeing, but we are free from all intellectually-formed delusions. Some delusions such as deluded doubt and wrong views are exclusively intellectually-formed and are therefore completely abandoned on the path of seeing. Other delusions such as anger and attachment may be either innate or intellectually-formed, and therefore they are not completely abandoned until the path of meditation. However, having realized emptiness directly, anger no longer arises, even though it has not been completely abandoned at this stage.

At the same time as attaining the Mahayana path of seeing we also reach the first ground of a Bodhisattva. A Bodhisattva on the first ground has many special qualities. For example, when we have reached this stage we experience no pain even if someone cuts up our body piece by piece. Having realized directly that we and our body are empty of inherent existence, being merely imputed by conception, we feel no more pain when our body is cut than when we see a tree being cut. A Bodhisattva on the first ground also possesses special qualities based on the number one hundred. For example, such a Bodhisattva can see a hundred Buddhas in the shortest instant, see a hundred aeons into the future and the past, and emanate a hundred bodies simultaneously. If we know the many qualities possessed by someone who has reached the path of seeing we shall understand that it is a very special attainment. However, as long as we remain on the Mahayana path of seeing we shall not be able to abandon all the obstructions

Ksitigarbha

preventing our full enlightenment. This is because our meditative equipoise on emptiness at this stage does not have the power to eliminate innate delusions nor the imprints of delusions. Therefore, while on the path of seeing we need to strengthen our direct realization of emptiness and strive to attain the higher Mahayana paths.

The way to practise the perfection of wisdom while on the Mahayana path of seeing is explained in the next section of the Sutra. This teaches that, having gained a direct realization of the emptiness of phenomena, we strengthen this realization by using eight objects as the bases of emptiness:

(1) The nature of phenomena
(2) The characteristics of phenomena
(3) The production of phenomena
(4) The cessation of phenomena
(5) The defilements of phenomena
(6) The separation from defilements of phenomena
(7) The decrease of phenomena
(8) The increase of phenomena

If we realize the emptiness of these eight bases we shall understand that phenomena lack all trace of inherent existence. Although the Sutra principally expresses the emptiness of these eight bases, it also implicitly teaches their conventional existence.

'Shariputra, like this all phenomena are merely empty' explains that, just like the nature of the five aggregates, the nature of all phenomena is empty of inherent existence. Each and every phenomenon has its own particular nature, but these natures exist only nominally; they are not inherently existent.

The phrase 'having no characteristics' does not mean that phenomena do not have any characteristics at all, but rather that they do not have inherently existent characteristics. In general, phenomena do have characteristics. The characteristics of phenomena are those features that enable us to distinguish one particular phenomenon from another. If we do not have a clear understanding of the characteristics of a phenomenon we may easily confuse it with others. Avalokiteshvara's words implicitly teach that we need to develop a clear understanding of the particular characteristics of phenomena – such as emptiness, virtuous actions, and non-virtuous actions – and apply this understanding to distinguish them correctly. If we fail to do this we shall experience serious difficulties.

Although it is important to be familiar with the characteristics of phenomena, all characteristics are empty of inherent existence. If a phenomenon's characteristics were inherently existent they would exist in themselves without depending on anything else, but this is not the case. For example, a house has many characteristics but none of them exists independently; they depend on the materials used in its construction, the work of its builders, and so forth. If we investigate carefully we can realize that all characteristics are dependent-related phenomena in this way and are therefore empty of inherent existence.

'They are not produced' does not mean that phenomena are not produced at all, but that the production of phenomena is not inherently existent. All impermanent phenomena such as our body are in fact produced from causes. The body that we have today was produced from the body we had yesterday. In this way the production of our body can be traced back to its original production from our parents' bodies. Similarly, our mind has arisen from previous moments of mind in a chain of production with no beginning. If we investigate we shall discover that the entire external world system and all the beings within it have been produced from causes. Also, our inner experiences of the world and our resultant happiness and unhappiness arise from causes, the principal causes being the previous continuum of our consciousness and our past actions. Implicitly the Sutra teaches that all impermanent phenomena, whether external or internal, are produced according to the principles of cause and effect.

However, the text mainly teaches that the production of phenomena is not inherently existent. We can be sure that production is empty of inherent existence because it quite clearly depends on causes and conditions – if the appropriate causes are not assembled, production does not take place. As discussed earlier, if something depends on other phenomena it is necessarily empty of inherent existence.

The phrase 'and do not cease' indicates that, like production, the cessation of phenomena is not inherently existent. Any phenomenon that is produced also ceases. We can consider the cessation of phenomena on two levels, gross and subtle. Examples of gross cessation are the death of a person and the breaking of a glass vase. In these cases the object changes to such an extent that there is no longer a suitable basis upon which to impute that object – a corpse is not suitable to be called a person, and fragments of glass are not suitable to be called a vase. Subtle cessation is the cessation of an object in a particular momentary state that leads to the production of the object in a new momentary state. For example, we at this moment are a different person from the person we were a moment ago because we undergo many subtle changes from one moment to the next. The person we are at this moment can come into existence only through the cessation of the person we were a moment ago. This type of cessation is subtle cessation because the change taking place in the object is so subtle that there continues to be a suitable basis for imputing the object. Thus, although the body and mind of a person called 'Peter' undergo subtle changes from one moment to the next, they remain a suitable basis for imputing Peter.

Indirectly this part of the Sutra teaches gross and subtle impermanence. The realization of subtle impermanence is itself a very powerful opponent to the arising of delusions. If we realize subtle impermanence we shall understand that the person who is reading this book today is not the person who went to bed last night. The person of yesterday had to cease for today's person to be produced, just as a seed must cease for a sprout to be formed. By realizing this we can prevent many delusions from arising. For example, if someone spoke harsh words to us yesterday, our realization of subtle impermanence will prevent us from becoming angry with that person today, because we shall realize that the person who spoke the harsh words and the person to whom the words were spoken have both ceased. The person who stands before us today is a fresh, new person; he or she is not the person who spoke to us yesterday. According to Dharma, if something is a functioning thing it is necessarily

newly developed. It is impossible for an impermanent phenomenon to remain for a second moment after its production; it disintegrates immediately. By remembering this we
can control not only our anger but also our other delusions
such as attachment, jealousy, and pride.

Although all impermanent things undergo cessation,
there is no inherently existent cessation. The cessation of an
object is merely an imputed phenomenon. For example, the
gradual transformation of a seed into a sprout involves the
cessation of the seed. However, there is no point at which
the seed from its own side ceases to exist. Both the seed and
the sprout are imputed phenomena, and the point at which
the seed has ceased and the sprout has been produced is
also imputed by our conception.

'They have no defilement' means that although phenomena do have defilements, they do not have inherently
existent defilements. 'Defilements' refers to faults such as
delusions, uncontrolled birth, and uncontrolled death.
Implicitly the text teaches that because defilements are a
source of suffering we should strive to abandon them. It is
therefore very important to know our own faults, but it is a
mistake to dwell on the faults of others. We are totally
responsible for our own faults and we must take the
responsibility to overcome them. If we have a good motivation and great skill we can sometimes help others to overcome their faults, but otherwise the faults of others should
not concern us. Buddha said 'A person who is aware of his
own faults is indeed wise.' Also the great Indian Teacher
Atisha said:

Do not look for faults in others, but look for faults in yourself, and purge them like bad blood.

Do not contemplate your own good qualities, but contemplate the good qualities of others, and respect everyone as a servant would.

This advice is very useful if we wish to control our minds. If we do not practise in this way we shall constantly see faults in others and develop anger, pride, and negative thoughts. If we look for faults in others we shall definitely find them; for example Devadatta, who was Buddha's cousin, even saw many faults in Buddha. Looking for faults in others merely disturbs our mind without producing any benefits, and therefore instead of looking for faults in others we should investigate our own faults and try to abandon them.

Although we have faults and defilements they are not inherently existent. If they were, we would have no possibility of overcoming them, because if something is inherently existent it exists independently and cannot be altered in any way. From our own experience we know that our faults can decrease if we apply the correct remedy. Through this slight experience we can understand that it is possible eventually to eradicate all our faults and thereby become a Buddha. All the faults that we possess are included in the two obstructions – delusion-obstructions and obstructions to omniscience. All our delusions, such as ignorance, anger, and attachment, are delusion-obstructions, and our imprints of delusions are obstructions to omniscience. Our delusion-obstructions principally prevent us from attaining liberation from samsara, and our obstructions to omniscience

principally prevent us from realizing all objects of knowledge directly and simultaneously. Only Buddhas have
completely overcome these two obstructions. Therefore,
anyone who wishes to become free from all faults and
endowed with all good qualities should develop the wish to
attain Buddhahood. It is possible to attain this state because
our defilements are not inherently existent but arise from
causes that can be removed.

The words 'and no separation from defilement' principally teach that separation from defilement is not inherently existent. Implicitly it also teaches that it is possible to
attain a separation from defilement that is dependently
existent. Such a separation is possible because every fault
has an opponent and therefore, in dependence upon its
opponent, we can abandon the fault.

Generally, when we apply an opponent to a fault we first
attain a temporary separation from the fault. For example,
we can temporarily prevent anger from arising by practising its opponent, patience; but the potential for anger to
arise will remain. It is not until we become a Superior being
that we begin to abandon faults permanently. Thereafter,
we progressively abandon faults until we attain Buddhahood, the state completely free from all defilements and
faults. If we abandon a fault permanently, in dependence
upon a superior path, we attain a true cessation. The temporary separation from a defilement through virtuous practices is the foundation for attaining a true cessation in the
future.

'They have no decrease' means that although a phenomenon may decrease, the decrease is not inherently existent.

We know from experience that phenomena may decrease or reduce in intensity. For example, at one moment we may experience very strong anger, but later that anger subsides. Also positive qualities of mind, such as faith and compassion, can degenerate if they are not nurtured. Similarly, external objects such as rivers, forests, and even mountains are also subject to decrease. We need to understand that it is the nature of all impermanent phenomena to decrease in this way, but we should also realize that the decrease is not inherently existent. If the decrease of phenomena were inherently existent it could not be affected by circumstances, and phenomena would be in a permanent state of decrease. We know that in fact phenomena can change from a state of decrease to a state of increase in dependence upon causes and conditions. This is a clear indication that the decrease is not inherently existent.

The words 'and no increase' teach that an increase in a phenomenon, like a decrease, is empty of inherent existence. It is the nature of all impermanent phenomena to undergo increase, but, as in the case of decrease, increase arises in dependence upon causes and conditions and is empty of inherent existence.

In summary, this section of the Sutra principally teaches that phenomena are totally devoid of inherent existence by revealing that the nature and the attributes of phenomena are themselves empty of inherent existence. As well as teaching the ultimate nature of phenomena, it implicitly teaches many aspects of their conventional nature, such as subtle impermanence, cause and effect, and the abandonment of defilements.

This part of Avalokiteshvara's answer explains how we should practise the perfection of wisdom while on the Mahayana path of seeing. It indicates that the principal object of meditation on the path of seeing is the emptiness of phenomena, and that we can strengthen our realization of the emptiness of phenomena by realizing that the eight objects, from the nature of phenomena to the increase of phenomena, are all empty of inherent existence. The answer also indicates that the mind that meditates on emptiness while on the path of seeing is a non-conceptual direct perceiver that is free from dualistic appearance, and thus the only object that appears to this mind is emptiness – no conventional objects appear at all. Thus, with respect to this mind, 'all phenomena are merely empty, having no characteristics.'

Sarvanivaranaviskambini

The Path of Meditation

'Therefore, Shariputra, in emptiness there is no form, no feeling, no discrimination, no compositional factors, no consciousness. There is no eye, no ear, no nose, no tongue, no body, no mentality; no form, no sound, no smell, no taste, no tactile object, no phenomenon. There is no eye element and so forth up to no mentality element and also up to no element of mental consciousness. There is no ignorance and no exhaustion of ignorance and so forth up to no ageing and death and no exhaustion of ageing and death. Likewise, there is no suffering, origin, cessation, or path; no exalted awareness, no attainment, and also no non-attainment.'

In this next part of the Sutra Avalokiteshvara explains the practice of the perfection of wisdom on the Mahayana path of meditation. Before discussing the meaning of his words it will be helpful to describe the way in which we attain the path of meditation and how the Bodhisattva progresses along this path.

When we first gain a direct realization of emptiness and reach the path of seeing, our meditative equipoise on emptiness is able to overcome our intellectually-formed delusions but does not have the power to overcome our innate delusions. We remain on the path of seeing until we develop the exalted awareness of meditative equipoise that acts as the direct antidote to the most gross level of innate delusions. When we develop this wisdom we have attained the path of meditation.

The root cause of innate delusions is innate self-grasping. Unlike intellectually-formed self-grasping, this is not acquired through adopting a mistaken philosophy but arises instinctively in all beings in samsara, including animals. Innate self-grasping is a mind that develops naturally and apprehends phenomena to be inherently existent. It gives rise to the basic motivating force of self-preservation in even the most primitive forms of animal life. As a result of this self-grasping we develop other innate delusions such as anger, attachment, and pride.

Each innate delusion can be considered as having nine degrees, or levels, ranging from a very gross level to a very subtle level. The names given to these nine levels of innate delusion, starting with the most gross, are as follows:

(1) Big-big
(2) Middling-big
(3) Small-big

(4) Big-middling

(5) Middling-middling

(6) Small-middling

(7) Big-small

(8) Middling-small

(9) Small-small

We abandon these nine levels of innate delusion progressively during the path of meditation. We should not consider them to be nine different entities, like, for example, nine separate fires of different sizes. Instead, they are nine strengths or degrees of the same entity, like a single fire that can range from a great blaze to a tiny flame.

A Bodhisattva on the path of meditation abandons the most gross level of innate delusions first and then progressively abandons the more and more subtle levels of the delusions. We can compare this process to washing very dirty clothes. When we start washing the clothes, the heaviest dirt is quickly removed. As we continue to rub and soak the clothes we are able to wash away the less obvious ingrained dirt. Finally, if we are persistent, we are able to remove even the most subtle stains and our clothes become clean and pure. Similarly, on the path of meditation a Bodhisattva begins by abandoning the most gross level of delusion and then removes the more subtle levels in stages.

We attain the path of meditation when, having already attained the path of seeing, we develop the meditative equipoise on emptiness that acts as the direct antidote to big-big innate self-grasping. At that moment we have left the path of seeing and have attained the uninterrupted path of the path of meditation that is the antidote to big-big innate delusions. This uninterrupted path abandons the big-big level of innate delusions. As soon as we have abandoned this level of delusion we have progressed to the corresponding released path of the path of meditation. This released path is within the same meditative equipoise as the uninterrupted path but is a mind that is released from big-big delusions.

When we emerge from this meditative equipoise on emptiness we are able to continue with our other activities and practices. We are still on the path of meditation but the strength of our innate delusions has been reduced to the middling-big level. We need to engage again in meditations on emptiness in order to develop the meditative equipoise that acts as the direct antidote to middling-big innate self-grasping. When we have developed this we have attained the uninterrupted path that abandons the middling-big level of innate delusions. Later within the same meditative equipoise we attain the corresponding released path, our innate delusions having been reduced to the small-big level. In this way we abandon all nine levels of innate delusion progressively.

Once we have abandoned the small-small level of innate delusions, we have completely eradicated all our delusions. We have then overcome delusion-obstructions and gained liberation from samsara. If we are following the Hinayana path we have become a Hinayana Foe Destroyer, or Arhat. If we are following the Mahayana path we have attained the eighth ground of a Superior Bodhisattva.

If we attain the eighth ground of a Superior Bodhisattva
we are still on the Mahayana path of meditation but we are
free from all delusions and their seeds. Before we can attain
full enlightenment, or Buddhahood, we need to abandon
also the imprints of our delusions, which are the obstructions to omniscience. As a result of these imprints we continue to experience dualistic appearance when we are not
engaged in meditative equipoise on emptiness, and this
prevents our knowing all phenomena directly and simultaneously. To remove these final obstructions to Buddhahood
we must continue to meditate on emptiness and strengthen
our realization. By doing so we successively abandon the
gross, subtle, and very subtle obstructions to omniscience.
When we abandon the gross obstructions to omniscience
we progress to the ninth ground, and when we abandon the
subtle obstructions to omniscience we progress to the tenth
ground. When we abandon the very subtle obstructions to
omniscience we attain full enlightenment, or Buddhahood.

The way to practise the perfection of wisdom on the path
of meditation is explained by the next part of Avalokiteshvara's answer. His answer reveals that on the path of
meditation we should continue to meditate on emptiness
with a mind in which all dualistic appearances have ceased.

The words 'Therefore, Shariputra, in emptiness there is
no form, no feeling, no discrimination, no compositional
factors, no consciousness' indicate that when a person on
the Mahayana path of meditation is engaged in meditative
equipoise on emptiness, the five aggregates do not appear
to his or her mind of meditative equipoise. The five aggregates are conventional truths and, like all conventional

truths, when they appear to the mind of any being except a Buddha they appear to be inherently existent. Thus, since a Superior Bodhisattva is not yet a Buddha, if the five aggregates appear to his or her mind, they appear falsely to be inherently existent. The mind of a Superior Bodhisattva engaged in meditative equipoise on emptiness, however, is free from all false appearances, and therefore it follows that the five aggregates do not appear to that mind. If they did appear to this unmistaken mind it would imply that their appearance as inherently existent is not false, but true!

The following section of the text from 'There is no eye, no ear …' up to '… no tactile object, no phenomenon' indicates that the twelve sources are also empty of inherent existence and likewise do not appear to the exalted awareness of meditative equipoise of a Superior Bodhisattva. The twelve sources are:

(1) Eye source
(2) Ear source
(3) Nose source
(4) Tongue source
(5) Body source
(6) Mentality source
(7) Form source
(8) Sound source
(9) Smell source
(10) Taste source
(11) Tactile object source
(12) Phenomena source

'Source', here, refers to the source of consciousness. The first six sources are the five sense powers and the mental power – the eye source, for example, being the eye sense power. Each of the six powers is the uncommon dominant condition of one of the six consciousnesses – the eye sense power, for example, being the uncommon dominant condition of eye consciousness. A power is called the 'dominant condition' of a consciousness because although other conditions are necessary for a consciousness to develop, it is principally through the force of its specific power that the consciousness arises. Without the respective power it is impossible for a particular consciousness to develop. For example, if there is no eye sense power, eye consciousness cannot be generated.

The five sense powers are physical sense powers and possess form. The eye sense power is the sense power associated with the eye organ that directly and specifically gives rise to eye consciousness. It is not the physical eye organ itself, because a blind person may possess a complete eyeball but he does not possess an eye sense power. Even in the case of a normally-sighted person, eye consciousness is not generated during sleep. This is because at that time the person's eye sense power has absorbed, even though the physical eye organ is still present.

The other four sense powers are similar to the eye sense power. The ear sense power functions specifically to generate ear consciousness. No person can hear a sound unless he develops an ear consciousness, and for the person to develop an ear consciousness he must possess an ear sense power. Similarly, a saucepan, for example, is unable to smell or taste the food put into it because it lacks a nose and tongue sense power and therefore cannot generate a nose or tongue consciousness. The fifth sense power, the body sense power, functions specifically to generate body consciousness, which is the consciousness that apprehends tactile objects such as roughness, smoothness, heat, and cold. Without a body sense power, sensations of touch cannot be experienced. Thus inanimate objects are insensitive to touch because they lack a body sense power. Also people who are partially paralysed may have a restricted ability to experience tactile objects as a result of their body sense power being impaired.

The sixth power, the mental power, is the power that functions specifically to generate mental consciousness. The mental power is itself a consciousness and as such does not possess form. It is therefore a mental power rather than a sense power possessing form. The mental power is rather more difficult to understand than the sense powers, but the way it functions can be illustrated by an example. If we look at a page of this book we apprehend the page with our eye consciousness in dependence upon our eye sense power. If we then close our eyes and recall the page to our mind we shall apprehend the page with our mental consciousness. Before the mental consciousness that actually apprehends the page can be generated, a previous consciousness must develop that causes our mind to turn towards remembering the page. This previous consciousness is the mental power with respect to the mental consciousness that apprehends the page. Every moment of mental consciousness must have a previous moment of consciousness as its mental power in order to be generated.

The last six of the twelve sources are called 'object sources' because they act as a source of consciousness by being the objects that appear to consciousness. The first of the six object sources, form source, does not refer to the aggregate of form but refers only to visual form, which is the object of eye consciousness. Sound source, smell source, taste source, and tactile object source are the respective objects of ear, nose, tongue, and body consciousness. The last of the six object sources, phenomena source, refers specifically to phenomena that appear exclusively to mental consciousness, such as permanent phenomena. The other five object sources can also appear to mental consciousness. For example, we can recall visual forms, sounds, and so forth with our mental consciousness – but these objects are not included within phenomena source.

Each moment of consciousness has an object that is its object condition. Just as consciousness cannot arise without a power as its dominant condition, neither can it arise without an object as its object condition. The six object sources act as the objects of the six consciousnesses and are therefore a necessary condition for consciousness to arise.

Avalokiteshvara's words teach that although the six powers and the six object sources are essential conditions for the generation of consciousness, they are not inherently existent. When it is stated that there is no eye, no ear, and so forth, it means that the twelve sources do not appear to the meditative equipoise of a Superior being. For such a mind all conventional appearances such as the twelve sources have dissolved into emptiness.

The next part of the text, from 'There is no eye element ... ' to '... no element of mental consciousness' refers to the eighteen elements:

 (1) Eye element
 (2) Ear element
 (3) Nose element
 (4) Tongue element
 (5) Body element
 (6) Mentality element
 (7) Form element
 (8) Sound element
 (9) Smell element
(10) Taste element
(11) Tactile object element
(12) Phenomena element
(13) Element of eye consciousness
(14) Element of ear consciousness
(15) Element of nose consciousness
(16) Element of tongue consciousness
(17) Element of body consciousness
(18) Element of mental consciousness

The eighteen elements are a comprehensive classification of all phenomena. There are many different ways in which phenomena can be categorized, for example into permanent and impermanent phenomena, or conventional truths and ultimate truths. The division into eighteen elements is a method of classifying phenomena in terms of their nature.

The first twelve elements are the twelve sources already described. The last six elements are the six consciousnesses that arise in dependence upon the twelve sources.

Through the meeting of the six objects and the six powers we develop the six consciousnesses. The objects, the powers, and the consciousnesses are mutually dependent. For example, if we have an eye sense power but there is no blue colour we shall not develop an eye consciousness seeing blue. However, if our eye sense power and the object blue do meet, then an eye consciousness seeing blue will develop. The same principle applies to the other consciousnesses.

Through internal investigation we can understand not only how the various consciousnesses develop but also what their functions and effects are. For example, our eye consciousness beholds various forms and this can function to produce various effects. When our eye consciousness sees beautiful forms it can cause us to generate desire, and when it sees unpleasant objects it can cause us to generate anger. In the case of ordinary beings, even if their eye consciousness perceives a neutral object it generally causes ignorance to arise in their mind. Thus for those who have not trained in Dharma, even the development of eye consciousness causes delusions to arise and so indirectly causes many problems. Eye consciousness also induces various feelings, and as a result we can later develop many distracting conceptual thoughts. This is a particular problem for those who wish to meditate seriously. Indeed, some sincere meditators may develop the thought that it would be better if they were blind! Then they would be unable to see anything and would develop fewer distractions during their meditation. Because our sense consciousnesses can give rise to distracting thoughts it is recommended that we go to a very isolated place to do serious meditation, particularly when we try to attain tranquil abiding.

A single object may be dependent on a collection of many elements. For example, an apple is composed of elements of form, smell, taste, tactile object, and so forth. Modern scientists have developed great skill in investigating the elements, or natures, of external objects. As a result they have been able to discover the various properties of matter and have applied this knowledge to change the environment and to create new materials, elaborate machines, and so forth. Most scientists are principally concerned with very detailed studies of the elements of form, sound, smell, taste, and tactile object, these being the objects of the five sense consciousnesses.

In a similar way, it is possible to study in detail the remaining elements, such as the subtle objects of mental consciousness and consciousness itself. We cannot study these elements using the same tools as those used to study the objects of the sense consciousnesses. Consciousness and subtle phenomena such as emptiness cannot be studied using microscopes, chemical analysis, or particle accelerators. The most effective tool to use is wisdom. Using our wisdom we can investigate the fine workings of the mind and discover the ultimate nature of phenomena. The understanding we acquire in this way will enable us to develop a peaceful, happy mind, and build the foundation for attaining liberation and enlightenment.

Avalokiteshvara's words implicitly teach the conventional nature of the eighteen elements and their importance in understanding the multiplicity of phenomena, but principally they teach that the eighteen elements are not inherently existent and do not appear to the meditative equipoise of a Superior being. Although the eighteen elements appear to be inherently existent, this appearance is false – in fact, the elements are merely imputed by conception.

The next part of Avalokiteshvara's answer, from 'There is no ignorance ... ' up to ' ... and no exhaustion of ageing and death', refers to two sets of twelve dependent-related links. The first set of twelve dependent-related links are links or stages in the process through which sentient beings remain trapped within samsara, taking one contaminated rebirth after another. These twelve links are as follows:

(1) Dependent-related ignorance
(2) Dependent-related compositional actions
(3) Dependent-related consciousness
(4) Dependent-related name and form
(5) Dependent-related six sources
(6) Dependent-related contact
(7) Dependent-related feeling
(8) Dependent-related craving
(9) Dependent-related grasping
(10) Dependent-related existence
(11) Dependent-related birth
(12) Dependent-related ageing and death

The dependent-related ignorance that is the first link is a specific type of ignorance. It is a mind of self-grasping that motivates a person to create an action that is the cause for taking rebirth in samsara. Such a mind is called 'ignorance' because it grasps phenomena as inherently existent through being ignorant of their true nature.

The second link, dependent-related compositional actions, is an action, or karma, that is the projecting cause for taking a rebirth in samsara. Since its effect is to project, or throw, us into a rebirth in samsara it is also called 'throwing karma'. Although a compositional action is motivated by the first link, dependent-related ignorance, it may be virtuous or non-virtuous depending on the intention accompanying it. A virtuous compositional action leads to a cyclic rebirth in one of the three higher realms, whereas a non-virtuous compositional action leads to a cyclic rebirth in one of the three lower realms.

The third link, dependent-related consciousness, does not refer to consciousness in general but only to the consciousness that receives the imprint of a dependent-related compositional action. Each compositional action, such as the non-virtuous action of killing, leaves an imprint upon our consciousness. This imprint remains in our continuum of consciousness as a seed-like potency until the circumstances arise that activate it to produce the effect of a rebirth in samsara.

The fourth link is dependent-related name and form. This link is the five aggregates of a person at the moment of rebirth – form being the form aggregate and name being the other four aggregates. We can take our own birth as an example. We took our present rebirth as a human being when our consciousness entered the fertilized ovum in our mother's womb. At that moment we comprised five rudimentary aggregates; our form aggregate was the physical form of the fertilized ovum, and the remaining aggregates of feeling and so forth were also present. Our five aggregates at that moment are an example of the fourth link, dependent-related name and form. The last four aggregates are called 'name' because they serve as a basis for naming or identifying a person even in the case of a person in the formless realm, who lacks a form aggregate.

Dependent-related six sources, which are the fifth link, are the five sense powers and the mental power when they first develop after rebirth. In the case of our present rebirth as a human being we had the mental power and body sense power from the moment of conception, but the remaining four sense powers of eye, ear, nose, and tongue were generated gradually as we developed in the womb.

The sixth link is dependent-related contact. Contact is a mental factor that accompanies every moment of consciousness. It arises from the coming together of an object, a sense power, and a consciousness. Its function is to perceive an object as pleasant, unpleasant, or neutral.

In dependence upon contact we develop the seventh link, dependent-related feeling. Whereas contact perceives an object as pleasant, unpleasant, or neutral, feeling is the mental factor that experiences the object as pleasant, unpleasant, or neutral. Whenever we cognize an object we generate a pleasant, unpleasant, or neutral feeling.

Dependent-related craving, the eighth link, is a particular form of attachment that nourishes, or activates, the potentiality to take our next rebirth that was left on our

Akashagarbha

consciousness by a previous dependent-related compositional action. This type of attachment occurs at the time of our death. Normally at that time we develop a strong attachment towards what we grasp as me, and towards our body, friends, possessions, and so forth. This craving activates the potential to take our next rebirth.

The ninth link is dependent-related grasping. This is also a type of attachment but it is more intense than craving. Craving can be compared with the strong desire to smoke a cigarette that is developed by someone who has recently given up smoking. Grasping is like that desire when it becomes so strong that it forces the person out of his house in search of a cigarette. Dependent-related grasping is the grasping that develops after dependent-related craving, and it activates more powerfully the potential to take our next rebirth.

The tenth link, dependent-related existence, is the mental factor intention that is induced by the previous links of craving and grasping. It is called 'existence' because it is the immediate cause of taking a new rebirth in cyclic existence; this is an example of the name of the effect being given to the cause. Intention in general is mental action, and the nature of intention determines whether a mind is virtuous or not. If the mental factor intention is virtuous, the mind that it accompanies is necessarily virtuous. Conversely, if the intention is non-virtuous, the mind it accompanies is also non-virtuous.

Although craving and grasping are delusions they can induce a virtuous mind at the time of death. For example, they can induce a mind that goes for refuge to, and prays to, holy beings. In such a case the tenth link, dependent-related existence, is a virtuous action and it is certain that an imprint left by a virtuous compositional action will be activated. The person will then take a fortunate rebirth as a human or a god. On the other hand, if the craving and grasping induce a non-virtuous mind, such as anger, then the tenth link is a non-virtuous action and a potential to take a rebirth in the lower realms will be activated.

The eleventh link is dependent-related birth. It refers to the moment when a consciousness takes a new existence. In the case of rebirth as a human being, dependent-related birth refers to the entry of a consciousness into a fertilized ovum in the mother's womb.

From the second moment of a new rebirth the process of ageing begins, and it continues until death. The final link, dependent-related ageing and death, is this process of ageing and death itself.

These twelve dependent-related links reveal the process whereby we remain chained to a cycle of uncontrolled rebirth and death with its associated sufferings. The fundamental cause of this uncontrolled process is the first link, ignorance, which is a mind that grasps at inherent existence. Under the control of ignorance we perform the virtuous or non-virtuous actions that are the cause for us to take rebirth in higher or lower realms of samsara. These actions are compositional actions, the second link. A compositional action leaves an imprint upon our mind, and the consciousness that receives this imprint is the third link. The first three links are sometimes called 'projecting causes' because they act as the cause to project us into a future uncontrolled rebirth. The three projecting causes are also called the 'distant causes' of rebirth because although they are the cause of a future rebirth, there may be many intervening lifetimes before that particular rebirth is actualized.

The next four links are called 'projected effects' and explain our development after having been projected into a new rebirth. The fourth link indicates that the basis of imputing our new identity is our new aggregates, name and form. In dependence upon our aggregates the fifth link, the six sources, are formed. The six sources are the six powers and as a result of these the sixth link, contact, arises. In dependence upon contact we develop pleasant, unpleasant, or neutral feelings, the seventh link.

The next three links indicate how the potential power to take our next rebirth is actualized, and they are therefore called 'actualizing causes'. These three links are also called 'close causes' of rebirth because they are the causes that immediately precede a rebirth. In dependence upon previous feelings, the eighth and ninth links, craving and grasping, arise as death approaches. These activate the potential to take our next rebirth, leading to the development of the tenth link, existence, which is the mental action that carries us towards our next rebirth.

The last two links are called 'actualized effects' because they are the effects of the actualizing causes. The three actualizing causes activate a particular potential to take rebirth, giving rise to the eleventh link, birth. As a result of birth within samsara the last link, ageing and death, occurs. The last two links also imply all the other sufferings of samsara, such as sickness, that occur between birth and death.

If we contemplate the twelve links in this sequence, from ignorance to ageing and death, we can understand the step-by-step development of cyclic rebirth and the sufferings associated with it. If we contemplate the twelve depend-ent-related links in reverse order, we can trace back the causes of our suffering. The last link combines two of the gross sufferings that we experience, ageing and death, but all our other sufferings are also implied. The cause of these sufferings is uncontrolled rebirth, the eleventh link. Birth results from the tenth link, existence, which is caused by grasping and craving, the ninth and eighth links. These two forms of attachment result from previous feelings, the sev-enth link. Feelings arise in dependence upon contact, the sixth link, which in turn depends upon the six sources, the fifth link. The six sources develop in dependence upon the five aggregates at the time of birth, which are the fourth link, name and form. The cause of taking these aggregates is an imprint carried by consciousness. The consciousness that received this imprint is the third link. The imprint on the consciousness is left by a compositional action, the sec-ond link. The root motivating force of compositional actions is ignorance, the mind that grasps at inherent existence. In this way we can trace back the cause of all suffering to ignorance, the first of the twelve links.

Thus, by contemplating the twelve links in reverse order we can realize that we experience suffering again and again because we have taken cyclic rebirth, and that the funda-mental cause of this miserable process is ignorance. Real-izing that the cause of all suffering is cyclic rebirth will lead us to develop the mind that wishes definitely to leave samsara. This mind is called the 'mind of definite emergence' or 'renunciation'. Realizing that ignorance is the root cause of cyclic rebirth we shall understand that the method to attain liberation from samsara is to dispel our ignorance. The direct antidote to ignorance is the wisdom that realizes emptiness. By persistent effort using correct methods we can develop this wisdom. If we then continue to meditate on emptiness with the motivation of renunciation and bodhichitta, our dependent-related ignorance, the first of the twelve links, will gradually diminish and eventually cease.

The complete cessation of dependent-related ignorance is the dependent-related exhaustion of ignorance. If we attain this exhaustion of ignorance our actions will no longer be controlled by delusions and therefore we shall attain the dependent-related exhaustion of compositional actions. This leads to the dependent-related exhaustion of consciousness and so forth, up to the dependent-related exhaustion of ageing and death. Thus, by attaining the exhaustion of ignorance we overcome cyclic rebirth and cut the continuum of suffering. The cessation of the continuum of suffering is liberation and is the state beyond sorrow, or nirvana. There is therefore a second set of twelve dependent-related links, from the exhaustion of ignorance to the exhaustion of ageing and death. The first set of twelve links from ignorance to ageing and death are called the 'twelve dependent-related links of the side of delusion', and the twelve links from the exhaustion of ignorance to the exhaustion of ageing and death are called the 'twelve dependent-related links of the perfectly purified side'. The former explain the development of cyclic rebirth and suffering, and the latter explain their cessation and the attainment of liberation.

The twelve links of the perfectly purified side are the mere cessation of the twelve links of the side of delusion. For example, dependent-related exhaustion of consciousness is not the cessation of consciousness in general, but the complete cessation of consciousness that receives the imprint of compositional actions. Similarly dependent-related exhaustion of feeling is merely the cessation of feelings that are contaminated by delusions. If we attain liberation we still have feelings, but these feelings are not contaminated and do not lead to craving and grasping at the time of death.

Having attained liberation we shall no longer be projected into a rebirth under the control of delusions, but nevertheless we experience uncontaminated rebirth. An uncontaminated rebirth does not have the nature of suffering and does not give rise to suffering in the future. Most Hinayana Foe Destroyers take an uncontaminated rebirth in a Pure Land and remain in a quiescent state of peace for a very long time. On the other hand, high Bodhisattvas continue to take rebirth among beings within samsara in order to benefit them. Such a rebirth is not contaminated, because it arises through the force of compassion and not through the force of delusions. If a high Bodhisattva takes rebirth as a human being, he or she will appear to others as an ordinary human being; but such a Bodhisattva is completely free from the sufferings of samsara and works joyfully for the sake of others.

By contemplating the twelve dependent-related links of the perfectly purified side our mind will be uplifted because we shall understand that we can completely abandon suffering and its causes by overcoming our ignorance that grasps at the inherent existence of phenomena.

Although extensive teachings on the conventional nature of the twelve dependent-related links are implied by the reference to them in the Sutra, principally the Sutra teaches that neither of the two sets of twelve links appears to the exalted awareness of meditative equipoise of a Superior being. They do not appear because they are conventional truths. Although an understanding of the twelve links has great value, we should realize that they are merely imputed phenomena, lacking inherent existence.

Avalokiteshvara goes on to say 'Likewise, there is no suffering, origin, cessation, or path'. This section is a reference to the four noble truths:

(1) True sufferings
(2) True origins
(3) True cessations
(4) True paths

All phenomena that have the nature of suffering are true sufferings. For example, the impure bodies and minds of all beings within samsara are true sufferings. These aggregates have the nature of suffering because they are produced as a result of actions contaminated by delusions. However, if something is a true suffering it is not necessarily an unpleasant feeling. For example, the pleasant feeling of a being enjoying the pleasures of a god realm develops as a result of previous virtuous actions and is consequently not a suffering, but nevertheless this mind is a true suffering. It is a true suffering because the pleasure experienced in the god realms is the result of contaminated virtuous actions motivated by self-grasping. Beings living in the god realms are still within samsara and their happiness contains within it the seed of suffering. Since such beings are controlled by delusions and previous contaminated actions, their life of pleasure will eventually cease and they must take rebirth again in the lower realms without choice. Thus the body and mind of a being in a god realm have the nature of suffering. The environments of beings within samsara are also true sufferings because these environments arise in dependence upon contaminated actions and delusions and give rise to the experience of suffering. Of the twelve dependent-related links, the six effects – name and form, six sources, contact, feeling, birth, ageing and death – are examples of true sufferings.

The second noble truth, true origins, is the main cause of true sufferings. If we investigate we find that all true sufferings are caused by delusions and the actions that are performed under the control of delusions. Therefore, these delusions and contaminated actions are true origins. Of the twelve dependent-related links, the six causes – ignorance, compositional actions, consciousness, craving, grasping, and existence – are true origins.

The third noble truth is true cessations. An actual true cessation is the ultimate nature of a mind that has attained the final cessation of any defilement or fault through the power of a true path. A true cessation is therefore not the final cessation of a fault itself, but is the emptiness of a mind that has attained a final cessation of a fault. However, because all minds are empty of inherent existence, if a person attains the final cessation of a fault he or she necessarily attains a true cessation. Because a true cessation is an emptiness of inherent existence it is an ultimate truth. An example of a true cessation is the emptiness of inherent existence of the released path of the path of seeing. The emptiness of this mind is a true cessation because this mind has attained the final cessation of intellectually-formed delusions through the power of a true path. Because true cessations arise in dependence upon true paths, which are possessed only by Superior beings, we cannot attain actual true cessations until after attaining the path of seeing.

The last of the four noble truths is true paths. Any mind of a Superior being that principally leads to the attainment of a true cessation is a true path. True paths are possessed only by Superior beings because only a mind that directly realizes emptiness has the power to lead to the final abandonment of a fault. The uninterrupted path of the path of seeing is an example of a true path. It is a true path because it is a mind of a Superior being and is the direct cause of the released path of the path of seeing, the emptiness of which is a true cessation.

The first two truths teach the nature and causes of samsara. The last two truths teach the nature of liberation from samsara and the way to attain it. In essence, all the teachings of Buddha are contained within the four noble truths but, like all phenomena, the four noble truths do not exist inherently; they are merely imputed by conception. This is the essential meaning of Avalokiteshvara's words.

We might interpret the words as indicating that none of the four noble truths appears to the exalted awareness of meditative equipoise of a Superior being. This leads to a contradiction because true cessations are ultimate truths and therefore can appear to this wisdom. We avoid this contradiction if we interpret 'cessation' in the text as meaning the mere cessation of true sufferings and true origins. Interpreted in this way, cessation does not refer to true cessation, which is an ultimate truth, but to a cessation that is a conventional truth and which therefore does not appear to the exalted awareness of meditative equipoise of a Superior being. Even though an actual true cessation can appear to the exalted awareness of meditative equipoise of a Superior being, it does not appear to that mind as inherently existent. The only object appearing to a Superior being who directly realizes a true cessation is the emptiness of inherent existence of a mind that has completely abandoned a fault.

The final part of this section of Avalokiteshvara's answer states 'no exalted awareness, no attainment, and also no non- attainment.' 'Exalted awareness' refers to the wisdom realizing emptiness possessed by a Superior being. 'Attainment' refers to virtuous qualities attained through the practice of spiritual paths. These attainments include temporary attainments such as the happiness of higher rebirths resulting from virtuous actions, and ultimate attainments such as the ten forces of enlightened beings. The ten forces are explained in *Joyful Path of Good Fortune*. 'Non-attainment' refers to those things that are to be abandoned or avoided, such as samsara, suffering, and delusions.

Avalokiteshvara's words teach that the wisdom of a Superior being that realizes emptiness is also empty of inherent existence. Furthermore, with respect to this exalted awareness of meditative equipoise of a Superior being, it is as though the wisdom itself does not exist. This is because the only object appearing to that mind is emptiness; the mind itself does not appear because it is a conventional truth. Similarly, attainments and non-attainments are conventional truths and do not appear to the exalted awareness of meditative equipoise of a Superior being. Like all phenomena they lack inherent existence, being merely imputed by conception.

In summary, this section of the Sutra explains how we should develop our practice of the perfection of wisdom while on the path of meditation. It explains that we should continue to meditate on the emptiness of inherent existence of phenomena with the exalted awareness of meditative equipoise that realizes emptiness directly. By continuing to meditate in this way, our direct realization of emptiness becomes increasingly powerful. Eventually it gains the power to act as the antidote to the most subtle levels of delusion, enabling us to eradicate our delusions completely. Then, if we continue to meditate with the wisdom of the Mahayana path of meditation, we can remove even the imprints of delusions, which are the obstructions to omniscience.

In his answer Avalokiteshvara describes the experience of a Bodhisattva on the path of meditation while meditating on emptiness. For the mind of that Bodhisattva, all conventional phenomena are absorbed and dissolved into emptiness so that the only object that appears during the meditation on emptiness is emptiness itself. It is as though no other phenomena exist. Even the mind that is apprehending emptiness is itself absorbed into emptiness and does not appear to the meditator. As a result the distinction between the mind and its object disappears.

The exalted awareness of meditative equipoise of a Superior being remains single-pointedly on emptiness and is mixed with emptiness like water poured into water. Beings who lack this wisdom develop many non-virtuous conceptual thoughts leading to numerous problems. When we realize emptiness directly, such non-virtuous conceptual thoughts no longer arise and our mind remains happy and peaceful, as described by Changkya Rölpai Dorje in *Song of Emptiness*:

> With reference to the face of the mother who is
>   separated from obstructions
> There is no trace of unevenness of any kind ...
> ... and there is smoothness, softness, and happiness.

'Mother' here refers to uncontaminated wisdom realizing emptiness directly. Because this wisdom lacks dualistic appearance it is 'separated from obstructions'.

The dissolution of ordinary appearances into emptiness is also an important practice of Secret Mantra. In Secret Mantra, or Tantra, methods are taught to develop very subtle minds that enable us to dissolve all phenomena into emptiness more easily. If we use these methods correctly we can overcome dualistic appearances more quickly than is possible using only the methods that are explained in Sutra teachings. A discussion of Secret Mantra practices, however, is beyond the scope of this book. For more detail see *Clear Light of Bliss* or *Tantric Grounds and Paths*.

As well as revealing the practice of emptiness on the path of meditation, this section of the Sutra also implicitly reveals many conventional aspects of the path to enlightenment. For example, the references to the twelve dependent-related links and the four noble truths implicitly teach the causes and effects of samsara and the methods to abandon these. Through these teachings Buddha helps us to overcome our confusion and develop our understanding.

If we reflect upon the value of the teachings contained in this Sutra we shall realize the great kindness of Buddha. Some people develop great respect for teachers because they demonstrate remarkable powers such as clairvoyance or the ability to levitate, but what lasting benefits do these demonstrations bring? If Buddha had only displayed miracle powers we would not be able to benefit greatly from these displays now. Fortunately, Buddha gave supreme teachings in order to dispel the confusion of sentient beings. These extensive and profound teachings have survived and have been translated into different languages. As a result we now have a good opportunity to study and practise his teachings and receive great benefits.

Even in a country like Tibet, which compared with western countries is materially very poor, people have gained important benefits through Buddha's teachings. Many Tibetans have developed wisdom in profound subjects, such as the nature of the mind, the causes of suffering, and the methods to attain liberation; and as a result they have attained a state of joy and peace, as well as the ability to help others overcome their problems. These attainments were possible because of the kindness of Buddha in giving his comprehensive teachings. In a similar way, regardless of our position in society, we too can apply Buddha's teachings to overcome our own problems and to help many other beings in this world.

The Path of No More Learning

'Therefore, Shariputra, because there is no attainment, Bodhisattvas rely upon and abide in the perfection of wisdom; their minds have no obstruction
and no fear. Passing utterly beyond perversity, they
attain the final nirvana. Also all the Buddhas who
reside perfectly in the three times, having relied
upon the perfection of wisdom, became manifest and
complete Buddhas in the state of unsurpassed, perfect, and complete enlightenment.'

Avalokiteshvara now explains how to attain the Mahayana
Path of No More Learning, which is the fifth and final
Mahayana path. Whereas the four previous Mahayana
paths are minds of Bodhisattvas that lead to higher spiritual
attainments, the Mahayana Path of No More Learning is a
mind that has accomplished the final, supreme attainment

Je Tsongkhapa

of full enlightenment. It is called the 'Path of No More Learning' because at this stage there are no more objects of knowledge or spiritual practices to be learnt. Upon attaining this path we become a fully enlightened Buddha, having overcome all deluded minds and their imprints and having perfected all positive qualities. There is no higher attainment possible than the state of Buddhahood, and therefore when we attain the Mahayana Path of No More Learning we have completed our spiritual training.

We attain the Mahayana Path of No More Learning by completing the previous path, the Mahayana path of meditation. As already described, while on the path of meditation we progressively abandon innate delusions and their imprints. The last stage of the path of meditation is the tenth ground of a Bodhisattva. If we have reached this stage we have already attained liberation from samsara, having overcome all our delusions. We have also eliminated the gross and subtle levels of the obstructions to omniscience so that only the very subtle obstructions to omniscience remain. Indeed, having attained the tenth ground we have already developed many extraordinary qualities of body, speech, and mind that are very similar to those of a Buddha. Finally, while on the tenth ground we develop a special meditative equipoise on emptiness that is the last uninterrupted path of the path of meditation. This uninterrupted path is the direct antidote to the very subtle obstructions to omniscience, and is called the 'vajra-like concentration of the tenth ground'. In the next moment we attain Buddhahood, so the vajra-like concentration is the last mind of a sentient being. When the vajra-like concentration overcomes the final obstructions to omniscience, we pass into a state in which all phenomena appear directly and simultaneously to us while our mind remains inseparably mixed with emptiness like water mixed with water. At that moment we have attained the Mahayana Path of No More Learning and have passed into the state of Buddhahood.

When we attain the Mahayana Path of No More Learning, our mind transforms into the Wisdom Truth Body of a Buddha. This Wisdom Truth Body is the resultant perfection of wisdom. Because this mind not only realizes emptiness directly, but also directly knows all phenomena simultaneously, it is omniscient wisdom. The mind of a Buddha sees all phenomena at the same time as clearly and directly as we are able to see the palm of our hand.

When our mind transforms into the Wisdom Truth Body of a Buddha, the emptiness of our mind transforms into the Nature Body of a Buddha – the Nature Body being the emptiness of inherent existence of a Buddha's omniscient mind. The Wisdom Truth Body and the Nature Body are the Truth Bodies of a Buddha.

Although the Truth Bodies of an enlightened being pervade everywhere, they lack form and cannot be perceived by sentient beings; they can only be perceived by Buddhas. Therefore, through the boundless wish to benefit others a Buddha manifests in the form of an Enjoyment Body. The Enjoyment Body of a Buddha can be perceived by Superior Bodhisattvas but not by beings who have not attained the Mahayana path of seeing. To benefit those other beings, countless Emanation Bodies arise from the Enjoyment Body and appear simultaneously throughout the universe. A

Buddha manifests Emanation Bodies spontaneously and effortlessly according to the needs and development of individual sentient beings.

The body and the mind of a Buddha are not different entities. Although the Enjoyment and Emanation Bodies of a Buddha have the aspect of form, their nature is wisdom. The bodies of a Buddha are manifestations of the Buddha's mind, just as ripples on the surface of water are manifestations of the water. In contrast, the body and mind of a sentient being are different entities. For example, our body has the nature of gross form and has developed from our parents' bodies, whereas the nature of our mind is clarity and cognizing and has developed from a quite different source, namely our previous mental continuum.

There are various types of Emanation Body. Buddha Shakyamuni, who appeared on this earth over two thousand five hundred years ago, is an example of a Supreme Emanation Body – an Emanation Body that performs the twelve principal deeds of a Buddha. Buddhas can also manifest as ordinary beings or even inanimate objects. How these emanations are perceived by other beings, and whether they are recognized as Emanation Bodies, depend upon the observers' accumulated merit. Merit accumulates through the power of performing virtuous actions and can be destroyed by performing non-virtuous actions. Just as we would not expect an animal to have recognized Buddha Shakyamuni as an enlightened being, because of the limitations of the animal's mind, so too a human being with little merit is unlikely to recognize an Emanation Body of a

Buddha, because of the lack of virtuous imprints within the person's mental continuum.

If we realize the conventional nature of phenomena we shall understand that our environment and how we experience it depend upon our mind and its potentialities. Thus, the way in which an animal perceives this world is very different from the way in which a human perceives it. Similarly, a person with great merit accumulated through virtuous actions over many lifetimes experiences the world very differently to a person with little merit. Since the appearance of our environment depends upon our mind, as our mind becomes purer the appearance of our environment also becomes purer. If we purify our mind sufficiently and accumulate appropriate virtuous imprints we shall be able to recognize the Emanation Bodies of enlightened beings. As our mind develops further and we attain the Mahayana path of seeing, we shall be able to perceive directly Buddhas in the form of their Enjoyment Body and receive teachings from them. Finally, when we attain the Mahayana Path of No More Learning we shall also be able to perceive the Truth Bodies of all the Buddhas.

This next section of the Sutra teaches the way in which a Bodhisattva attains the Path of No More Learning, or Buddhahood. The section begins with the words 'Therefore, Shariputra, because there is no attainment'. This reiterates that the attainments of a Bodhisattva, in particular the attainment of the Path of No More Learning, are empty of inherent existence. Even the attainment of Buddhahood does not exist in itself but is merely imputed by mind. If the attainments of a Bodhisattva were inherently existent they would exist independently without relying upon causes. In this case it would follow that a person would either possess the attainments, including Buddhahood, from the very beginning without effort, or be unable to accomplish these attainments whatever methods were used and regardless of the effort made. In reality the attainments of a Bodhisattva lack inherent existence. It follows that we cannot accomplish these attainments without applying the appropriate methods and effort, but on the other hand it is only because the attainments are empty of inherent existence that we can accomplish them at all.

Thus, this part of the text teaches that because the attainments of a Bodhisattva are empty of inherent existence Bodhisattvas strive to accomplish them by using reliable methods. The principal method they use is indicated by the words 'Bodhisattvas rely upon and abide in the perfection of wisdom'. In general, by relying upon the causal perfection of wisdom Bodhisattvas accomplish their progressive attainments as already described. In particular, the text refers to the final attainment of the Path of No More Learning, and so, here, 'the perfection of wisdom' refers specifically to the vajra-like concentration of the tenth ground. By relying upon and abiding in this concentration on emptiness the Bodhisattva accomplishes the ultimate attainment – Buddhahood. The phrase 'their minds have no obstructions and no fear' indicates that in this state they have overcome the two obstructions and therefore have nothing to fear.

'Passing utterly beyond perversity, they attain the final nirvana' indicates that by overcoming all faults a Bodhisattva completes his or her attainment of Buddhahood, thereby attaining the final and ultimate nirvana, the 'state beyond sorrow'.

Avalokiteshvara concludes this part of his answer to Shariputra with the words 'Also all the Buddhas who reside perfectly in the three times, having relied upon the perfection of wisdom, became manifest and complete Buddhas in the state of unsurpassed, perfect, and complete enlightenment.' This summarizes how enlightenment is attained through relying upon the perfection of wisdom of the five Mahayana paths.

'All the Buddhas who reside perfectly in the three times' refers to the Buddhas of the past, present, and future. In this present Fortunate Aeon, one thousand Buddhas will appear and perform the twelve principal deeds – Buddha Shakyamuni being the fourth and most recent of these. Since Buddha Shakyamuni's teachings are still available to us, he and all those who have attained Buddhahood through his teachings are called 'present Buddhas'. The three previous Buddhas of this aeon were Krakuchchanda, Kanakamuni, and Kashyapa. They appeared in this world system during earlier ages, and, like Buddha Shakyamuni, they turned the Wheel of Dharma, giving extensive and profound teachings. However, the lineage of their teachings faded and disappeared from this world long before the time of Buddha Shakyamuni. Therefore these three Buddhas and those who attained enlightenment as a result of their teachings are called 'past Buddhas'. Eventually the teachings of Buddha Shakyamuni will also be lost to the ordinary beings of this world, and the world will enter a dark period when no pure teachings are available. This dark age will be ended by the appearance of the next Buddha, Maitreya. Buddha Maitreya and the remaining nine hundred and ninety-five Buddhas of this aeon are called 'future Buddhas'. The reason they are called future Buddhas is not because they will attain Buddhahood in the future, but because in the future they will manifest in this world in the form of a Supreme Emanation Body and give teachings. In fact, Buddha Maitreya and the other future Buddhas of this aeon have already attained enlightenment.

The method used by the Buddhas of the past, present, and future to attain enlightenment is explained by the words 'having relied upon the perfection of wisdom, became manifest and complete Buddhas in the state of unsurpassed, perfect, and complete enlightenment.' This explains that the past, present, and future Buddhas attained enlightenment by relying upon the perfection of wisdom. Here, ' the perfection of wisdom' refers to the causal perfection of wisdom and the textual perfection of wisdom. The causal perfection of wisdom includes the wisdom realizing emptiness possessed by Bodhisattvas on the Mahayana paths of accumulation, preparation, seeing, and meditation. By relying upon the practice of the perfection of wisdom on these paths, the Bodhisattva attains the Mahayana Path of No More Learning, the omniscient wisdom of a Buddha. The textual perfection of wisdom is the Sutras and texts that reveal and explain the actual perfection of wisdom of the five Mahayana paths.

All the thousand Buddhas of this great aeon, and all others who have attained full enlightenment, have done so in dependence upon the five Mahayana paths. There is no other method to attain enlightenment apart from the practice of these paths; even the very advanced practices of Secret Mantra are contained within them. To progress along the Mahayana paths the Buddhas of the three times relied upon the perfection of wisdom. Likewise, anyone who wishes to attain Buddhahood in the future must rely upon the perfection of wisdom in the same way.

This concludes the explanation of Avalokiteshvara's answer that is intended for those with minds of lower faculties. In his answer Avalokiteshvara has explained the practice of the perfection of wisdom on the first four Mahayana paths, and how to attain the fifth Mahayana path, the omniscient wisdom of a Buddha.

The Mantra and Exhortation

'Therefore, the mantra of the perfection of wisdom, the mantra of great knowledge, the unsurpassed mantra, the equal-to-the-unequalled mantra, the mantra that thoroughly pacifies all suffering, since it is not false, should be known as the truth. The mantra of the perfection of wisdom is proclaimed:

TAYATHA OM GATE GATE PARAGATE PARASAMGATE
BODHI SÖHA'

This section of Avalokiteshvara's answer to Shariputra again explains how someone who has entered the Mahayana lineage should engage in the practice of the perfection of wisdom, but in this case the explanation is intended for those with particularly sharp mental faculties. Avalokiteshvara explains the practice of the five Mahayana paths by

The mantra of the perfection of wisdom

proclaiming the mantra of the perfection of wisdom. Only those with higher faculties are able to understand how to attain and practise the five paths simply through hearing the words of the mantra.

This does not imply that the previous explanation by Avalokiteshvara of how to practise the perfection of wisdom is easy to understand. The perfection of wisdom is a profound subject and cannot be understood without first receiving instruction and then applying effort to contemplate and meditate on it. Nevertheless, the explanation in terms of the mantra is much more concise than the previous explanation, and consequently sharper faculties are required to understand its meaning.

Avalokiteshvara begins this part of his answer by explaining the good qualities of the perfection of wisdom. The phrase 'Therefore, the mantra of the perfection of wisdom' refers to the perfection of wisdom as a mantra. In general, 'mantra' means 'protection for the mind'. Here, the perfection of wisdom is called a 'mantra' because it principally protects our mind from the two obstructions and the fears associated with them. The perfection of wisdom is called 'the mantra of great knowledge' because it knows the great seal, or emptiness. Also, the perfection of wisdom is called 'the unsurpassed mantra' because there is no mantra that is superior to the perfection of wisdom. Furthermore, it is called 'the equal-to-the-unequalled mantra' because there is no other mantra that is even equal to the perfection of wisdom. The perfection of wisdom is also 'the mantra that thoroughly pacifies all suffering' because through the sincere practice of the perfection of wisdom sentient beings are able to eliminate all their sufferings completely. 'Since it is not false, should be known as the truth' teaches that we should understand that the perfection of wisdom is non-deceptive. The perfection of wisdom protects us from all fears and pacifies all our suffering, and therefore it will never deceive us.

'The mantra of the perfection of wisdom is proclaimed' introduces the explanation of how to practise the perfection of wisdom. The explanation is in the form of the mantra: 'TAYATHA OM GATE GATE PARAGATE PARASAMGATE BODHI SÖHA'. This mantra, retained in the original Sanskrit, explains in very condensed form the practice of the five Mahayana paths, which we attain and complete in dependence upon the perfection of wisdom.

'TAYATHA' means 'it is like this' and indicates that whoever belongs to the Mahayana lineage and wishes to practise the paths of the perfection of wisdom should practise as follows.

The Sanskrit syllable 'OM' is composed of the three Sanskrit letters A, U, and M. In this case, these represent the body, speech, and mind of the person who is travelling to great enlightenment. In some texts this OM does not appear in the mantra, but since it is included in many authoritative commentaries to the Sutra I personally feel it is good to include this syllable here. Also, in many monasteries in Tibet there was a practice of reciting the mantra of the perfection of wisdom by a great assembly of monks to avert hindrances, and normally on these occasions OM was recited as part of the mantra.

The first 'GATE' means 'go'. This does not mean that we should go to an external place, but teaches that through generating bodhichitta we should go, or proceed, to the Mahayana path of accumulation. Having done this, we should practise the stages of the paths of method and wisdom of the path of accumulation.

The second 'GATE' again means 'go', and teaches that, having improved the stages of the paths of method and wisdom of the path of accumulation, we should go to the Mahayana path of preparation. Having reached this second Mahayana path, we should practise the stages of the paths of method and wisdom of the path of preparation.

'PARAGATE' means 'perfectly go', and teaches that we should not remain on the path of preparation permanently. Having improved the stages of the paths of method and wisdom of the path of preparation, we should go to the Mahayana path of seeing, the third path of the path to great enlightenment. We 'perfectly' go to the path of seeing because the path of seeing is a superior path beyond ordinary paths. Having attained the Mahayana path of seeing, we need to practise the stages of the paths of method and wisdom of this third Mahayana path.

'PARASAMGATE' means 'perfectly and completely go', and teaches that we should also not remain on the path of seeing. Having progressed in the stages of the paths of method and wisdom of the path of seeing, we should go to the Mahayana path of meditation, the fourth path of the path to great enlightenment. 'Perfectly and completely' go indicates that the Mahayana path of meditation is not only beyond ordinary paths, but also superior to the path of seeing, and therefore we need to progress to this path. Having done this, we need to practise the stages of the paths of method and wisdom of the Mahayana path of meditation.

'BODHI' means 'enlightenment'. This teaches that we must complete the practice of the stages of the paths of method and wisdom of the path of meditation, and attain the fifth and final Mahayana path, the Mahayana Path of No More Learning. When we reach this path, we have attained great enlightenment.

'SÖHA' means 'build the foundation'. Here it teaches that initially we should build the foundation of the path of accumulation. Then gradually we should build the foundation of the path of preparation, and so forth, until we attain final enlightenment, or Buddhahood.

In summary, this mantra teaches how to practise the perfection of wisdom that is the five Mahayana paths. Anyone who wishes to attain great enlightenment should practise these five paths progressively, successively, and completely.

In the beginning, through contemplating the twelve dependent-related links we should realize that as long as we remain within samsara we shall experience gross or subtle suffering unceasingly, instead of the pure happiness that our mind is capable of experiencing. Contemplating in this way, we shall understand that samsara is like a prison and we shall naturally develop the thought to use our present human life to attain liberation from it. This wish definitely to escape from samsara is the mind of renunciation.

Having cultivated the mind of renunciation, we should observe other sentient beings and realize that, like us, they wish to experience happiness, but like us they are trapped within samsara experiencing suffering again and again. Even the most fortunate humans, such as those with great wealth and fine bodies, cannot find lasting happiness within samsara, and inevitably experience the sufferings of ageing, sickness, death, and so forth. The suffering of less fortunate beings is all too obvious. Through contemplating the suffering of others we shall develop the thought of how wonderful it would be if all sentient beings were free from suffering and its causes. When this thought arises sincerely in us and is directed to all sentient beings without exception, we have developed the mind of great compassion.

After generating the mind of great compassion we should contemplate that we ourself must take responsibility to free all sentient beings from their suffering, just as a loving mother takes responsibility to care for her sick child. We shall then consider how we can develop the ability to lead all sentient beings from their suffering. We shall realize that only a Buddha has this ability because only a Buddha has omniscient wisdom and perfect skilful means to benefit others. Having realized this, the thought will arise that we must go to the Mahayana path of accumulation and then progress to the Mahayana paths of preparation, seeing, and meditation, and finally, in dependence upon the vajra-like concentration of the path of meditation, attain full enlightenment. By thinking in this way we should try to generate bodhichitta.

With the motivation of bodhichitta we should train in and practise the four profundities that were explained earlier. As our realization of the two truths deepens we shall actually progress from one Mahayana path to the next in the manner taught by the mantra of the perfection of wisdom.

Kadampa Geshes taught a method of reciting the mantra of the perfection of wisdom while visualizing the female Buddha Prajnaparamita in order to avoid obstacles and overcome hindrances. There is also a system of giving an empowerment of the Great Mother Prajnaparamita. In the final chapter a description is given of practices to overcome obstacles involving the recitation of both the *Essence of Wisdom Sutra* and the mantra of the perfection of wisdom. Here a brief explanation is given of a short practice involving just the recitation of the mantra.

At the beginning of this practice we develop compassion towards all sentient beings, thinking how wonderful it would be if they were freed from all their sufferings. Then we generate a strong motivation that we shall certainly practise the Mahayana paths from the path of accumulation to the Path of No More Learning for the sake of all sentient beings. With this motivation we recite the mantra of the perfection of wisdom, TAYATHA OM GATE GATE PARAGATE PARASAMGATE BODHI SÖHA, while remembering that all phenomena are empty of inherent existence. We should repeat this mantra as many times as we can. At the end of this recitation we pray that through the power of reciting this mantra all living beings including ourself may be freed from all harm and interferences. This prayer dedicates the benefits of the recitation.

In general, the motivation that precedes a virtuous action and the dedication that follows are a very important part of spiritual practice because they largely determine the effect of the action. It is also important that during the recitation practice we recall our understanding of emptiness. If we seriously and sincerely recite the mantra in this manner as a daily practice, it will act as a very powerful method to eliminate obstacles and hindrances, such as harm by others and sickness.

THE EXHORTATION TO PRACTISE THE
PERFECTION OF WISDOM

'Shariputra, a Bodhisattva, a Great Being, should train in the profound perfection of wisdom like this.'

With these words Avalokiteshvara exhorts Bodhisattvas and all others who aspire to attain great enlightenment to train in the profound perfection of wisdom as he has described. Those wishing to attain Buddhahood should attain successively the five Mahayana paths, progressing from path to path in dependence upon the practice of the perfection of wisdom as already explained. Without first attaining the Mahayana path of accumulation we cannot attain the Mahayana path of preparation. Likewise, we cannot jump to the path of seeing without having practised the path of preparation. Just as climbing a staircase one step at a time will definitely lead us to the top of a building, so the successive practice of each Mahayana path will definitely lead to the highest attainment of Buddhahood.

The principal wish of a Bodhisattva is to accomplish the happiness and welfare of all sentient beings, and in recognition of this supremely altruistic motivation a Bodhisattva is called a 'Great Being'. A Bodhisattva realizes that to fulfil this wish he or she must attain full enlightenment, for without omniscient wisdom it is not possible to work perfectly for the welfare of each and every sentient being; and so a Bodhisattva strives to attain full enlightenment in order to benefit others. Anyone who is seeking full enlightenment in this way should gradually practise the profound perfection of wisdom. In truth, this means that anyone who seeks full enlightenment should train in profound emptiness.

Buddha's Approval and the Promise to Practise

THE APPROVAL OF THE ANSWERS BY BUDDHA

Then the Blessed One arose from that concentration and said to the Superior Avalokiteshvara, the Bodhisattva, the Great Being, that he had spoken well: 'Good, good, O Son of the lineage. It is like that. Since it is like that, just as you have revealed, in that way the profound perfection of wisdom should be practised, and the Tathagatas will also rejoice.'

In this section of the Sutra Buddha expresses his approval of the answer given by Avalokiteshvara to Shariputra's question.

As explained earlier, both the question of Shariputra and the answer given by Avalokiteshvara were developed through the power and inspiration of Buddha. In truth, therefore, the answer to Shariputra's question 'How should a Son of the lineage train who wishes to engage in the practice of the profound perfection of wisdom?' was given by Buddha himself.

Je Phabongkhapa

In the *Perfection of Wisdom Sutra in One Hundred Thousand Lines* it is said that Dharma is revealed by the disciples of Buddha through the power of Buddha, and this is likened to the way in which all the waters of this world developed through the power of the naga king dwelling in Lake Manasarowar. Traditionally it is said that the source of all the rivers and waters of this world developed through the power of this king. Through his power the clouds formed and then rain fell, giving rise to rivers and oceans. As well as depending upon the power of the naga king, the development of rivers and so forth depends upon many external conditions such as the generation of water vapour and the formation of clouds. Also, beings experience water in this world because of their collective karma. If sentient beings on this earth had not created the cause to enjoy water, they would not experience water, whatever the power of the naga king. Indeed, there are many unfortunate beings in this world who live in environments that are almost totally devoid of water. Thus, water develops in dependence upon the assembly of many causes and conditions.

Just as the rivers and waters of this world arose through the power of the naga king, so the question of Shariputra and the answers by Avalokiteshvara arose through the power of Buddha. Again, this does not imply that it was only through the power of Buddha that the question and answers were spoken. It was also a necessary condition that those gathered had created the collective karma to receive these teachings.

These examples illustrate the general principle of the interdependence of phenomena. All the flowers, fruits, trees, and plants of this world grow in dependence upon water, and the formation of this water depends upon the power of the naga king. Likewise the instruction in Dharma that we receive depends upon the teachings of the disciples of Buddha, and ultimately upon the power of Buddha himself. Nothing develops through its own power; everything that is produced develops through the assembly of appropriate causes and conditions.

'Then the Blessed One arose from that concentration': the concentration that is referred to is the concentration called 'Profound Illumination' that was mentioned at the beginning of the Sutra. Because of the special qualities of Buddha's mind, he was able to inspire the speech of Shariputra and Avalokiteshvara and be aware of all that was said while remaining absorbed in this concentration on emptiness. Similarly, although Buddha outwardly appeared to arise from his concentration, his mind did not abandon the meditative equipoise on emptiness. In general the minds of Buddhas remain continuously in meditative equipoise on emptiness even while they are performing their various actions of body, speech, and mind. This ability to perform diverse actions while remaining in meditative equipoise on emptiness is a quality possessed only by Buddhas.

'And said to the Superior Avalokiteshvara, the Bodhisattva, the Great Being, that he had spoken well: Good, good, O Son of the lineage': in this way Buddha indicated that he was very pleased with the answer given by Avalokiteshvara.

'"It is like that. Since it is like that, just as you have revealed, in that way the profound perfection of wisdom should be practised"': this reveals that the explanation given by Avalokiteshvara was in complete accordance with Buddha's own view. With these words Buddha confirms that anyone who wishes to attain enlightenment through engaging in the practice of the profound perfection of wisdom should practise the stages of the paths revealed in Avalokiteshvara's answer.

'"And the Tathagatas will also rejoice."': 'Tathagata' is a Sanskrit word meaning 'one gone to thatness', and is an epithet of a Buddha. These words of Buddha can be interpreted in two ways. The first interpretation is that all the Buddhas join Buddha Shakyamuni in rejoicing in the words spoken by Avalokiteshvara, indicating that the answer given accords with the intention of all the Buddhas. The second interpretation is that if beings practise the perfection of wisdom as described in this Sutra, all the Buddhas will rejoice.

THE FOLLOWERS ARE PLEASED AND TAKE
THE TEACHINGS TO HEART

When the Blessed One had said this, the Venerable Shariputra, the Superior Avalokiteshvara, the Bodhisattva, the Great Being, and that entire circle of disciples as well as the worldly beings – gods, humans, demi-gods, and spirits – were delighted and highly praised what had been spoken by the Blessed One.

When Buddha expounded the extensive *Perfection of Wisdom* Sutras on Massed Vultures Mountain, there were many Bodhisattvas who attended, such as Avalokiteshvara, Manjushri, and Maitreya. There were also many Hinayana Hearers present, such as Shariputra, Subhuti, and Ananda. In addition to these highly realized disciples there were many worldly beings who came to listen to these teachings, such as gods from the form realm, gods from the desire realm, demi-gods, human beings, and spirits. This assembly of beings were also present when the *Essence of Wisdom Sutra* was expounded. As a result of hearing this Sutra, all these beings were greatly pleased, praising what had been spoken and taking the teachings to heart.

Conclusion

The meaning of the *Essence of Wisdom Sutra* has now been explained. Principally the Sutra gives advice to Mahayana practitioners who wish to engage in the practice of the perfection of wisdom. The Sutra reveals the meaning of the perfection of wisdom, and explains how to develop and enhance this wisdom.

If we are a Mahayana practitioner, or aspire to become one, our main aim is to attain enlightenment for the benefit of all sentient beings. To attain enlightenment we need to practise the stages of the paths of method and wisdom revealed by Avalokiteshvara through the power of Buddha. First we must develop the mind of renunciation, the determination definitely to leave samsara. Then through contemplating the suffering of others we need to develop great compassion and the precious mind of enlightenment. When we attain the mind of enlightenment we attain the first Mahayana path, the path of accumulation. We then need to progress from path to path until we attain the final Mahayana path, the Path of No More Learning.

Yongdzin Trijang Dorjechang

Our progress along the five Mahayana paths depends upon cultivating the corresponding five stages of the perfection of wisdom, culminating in the omniscient wisdom of a Buddha. Therefore, the main purpose of studying, contemplating, and meditating on the *Essence of Wisdom Sutra* is to develop these five stages of the perfection of wisdom in our own mental continuum.

Having gained some understanding of emptiness and the perfection of wisdom it can be very helpful to recite the *Essence of Wisdom Sutra* or just the perfection of wisdom mantra. If we do this recitation with the strong motivation to complete the five Mahayana paths it will help us to accomplish our wish.

We know that we ourself face continual problems and difficulties; and if we investigate we shall discover that there is not a single sentient being who is completely free from all harm and hindrances. We can use the recitation of the *Essence of Wisdom Sutra* as a method to overcome the hindrances that afflict both ourself and others. A practice to do this is described in the final chapter.

It is stated in many texts that we can purify our non-virtuous actions through reciting the Sutras of Buddha. Thus, the recitation of the *Essence of Wisdom Sutra* can also be used for this purpose. As with other methods of purification, we should do this practice in conjunction with the four opponent powers.

Another benefit of reciting the Sutra is that we thereby increase our collections of merit and wisdom. The collection of merit includes anything that principally assists the attainment of the Form Body of a Buddha, and the collection of wisdom includes anything that principally assists the attainment of the Truth Body of a Buddha. All four bodies of a Buddha are included in the Form Body and the Truth Body: the Form Body includes the Enjoyment Body and Emanation Bodies, and the Truth Body includes the Wisdom Truth Body and the Nature Body. Because the Form Body and the Truth Body arise from the collections of merit and wisdom respectively, a Buddha is said to be born from the two collections. Therefore, if we wish to be born as a Buddha we need to accumulate these two collections. Reciting the *Essence of Wisdom Sutra* increases in particular our collection of wisdom. Of the two collections, the collection of wisdom is much stronger because it is not destroyed by anger whereas our collection of merit can be destroyed in this way.

It can be beneficial to recite this Sutra aloud sometimes so that other beings such as animals and birds can hear. Although animals like our pet dogs and cats have no opportunity to practise Dharma in their present life, they may have many imprints upon their mind of virtuous actions performed in previous lives. Hearing the words of this Sutra can help to activate these virtuous imprints and place positive potentialities on their minds. There is a story that a pigeon used to overhear Vasubandhu reciting a Sutra. As a result of this, when the pigeon died it was reborn as a human being, and as a child could recall his previous life and spoke of the Master Vasubandhu. This child went on to study Dharma and became the great Buddhist scholar known as 'Stirmati'. In his previous incarnation as a pigeon he had many positive imprints from previous lives, and through hearing Vasubandhu reciting the Sutra these imprints were activated, helping him to achieve a human rebirth. In a similar way, if we recite the *Essence of Wisdom Sutra* aloud with a good motivation it will be of benefit to those who hear it.

Generally, the purpose of all the practices that we need to complete our passage to enlightenment are included within these two – to abandon obstacles (to purify negativities and overcome hindrances) and to increase the two collections of merit and wisdom. Through studying, contemplating, and meditating upon the *Essence of Wisdom Sutra*, and by reciting its words and mantra, we can accomplish both these purposes. Therefore, if we wish to progress towards great enlightenment we should abandon hesitation and doubt and joyfully engage in these practices.

Geshe Kelsang Gyatso Rinpoche

A Method to
Overcome Hindrances

In this chapter a method is described to overcome hindrances through the recitation of the *Essence of Wisdom Sutra* together with the contemplation of emptiness. The chapter is divided into three sections:

(1) An introduction to hindrances
(2) Illustrations of the practice of the Sutra
(3) The actual practice to overcome hindrances

AN INTRODUCTION TO HINDRANCES

In general, anything that prevents the achievement of happiness can be called an 'obstacle' or 'hindrance'. Throughout their lives ordinary beings experience unending hindrances preventing the attainment of the happiness that they seek. All these hindrances can be classified as either external or internal.

External hindrances are those hindrances that arise from causes outside our body and mind. They may arise from animate or inanimate objects. The harm we receive from malevolent humans and wild animals are examples of external hindrances arising from animate objects. Inanimate objects can also cause great harm. For example, the four external elements of earth, water, fire, and wind can give rise respectively to earthquakes, floods, destructive fires, and hurricanes. These are external hindrances arising from inanimate objects.

Internal hindrances arise from causes within our body and mind. Like the external environment our body can be considered as composed of the four elements of earth, water, fire, and wind, which, broadly, have the nature of solidity, liquidity, heat, and movement, respectively. If these four internal elements are in a state of harmonious equilibrium our body is healthy. When they are out of balance our body experiences a variety of problems and diseases. It has been said that our body is like a basket containing four poisonous snakes that constantly wrestle with each other. In that situation, if one snake becomes stronger than the rest it will overcome and kill the others. In a similar way, the very delicate balance between the four internal elements that is necessary for our body to be healthy can easily be disturbed by one element becoming dominant. Because of this the internal elements of our body are a source of recurring hindrances in the form of ill health, disease, and pain.

Our mind can also be the source of internal hindrances. If our mind is filled with negative thoughts and emotions we shall experience great harm and suffering as a result. In fact, the greatest obstacles to achieving happiness are the three mental poisons of desirous attachment, hatred, and ignorance.

These prevent our achieving a peaceful mind, and also destroy whatever happiness we may have gained.

We can now consider the main sources of interference that hinder our progress to liberation and enlightenment. These can be summarized as the four maras, 'mara' being a Sanskrit word meaning 'demon'. The four maras are:

(1) The mara of the delusions
(2) The mara of the aggregates
(3) The mara of the Lord of Death
(4) Devaputra mara

THE MARA OF THE DELUSIONS

Delusions are unpeaceful states of mind that directly or indirectly give rise to the suffering of sentient beings. They are included within true origins, the second noble truth. The three principal delusions are the three mental poisons already mentioned – desirous attachment, anger, and ignorance. Together with deluded pride, deluded doubt, and deluded view, they constitute the six root delusions from which all other delusions stem.

All the suffering that we experience arises as a result of our delusions and the actions we create under their influence. As well as disrupting our temporary happiness and peace, delusions also hinder our progress towards the ultimate happiness of liberation and enlightenment. Through considering the twelve dependent-related links we can understand that we cannot gain complete liberation from suffering unless we overcome ignorance, the source from which all other delusions spring. Because delusions are a

main obstacle to the attainment of liberation and enlightenment, they are called a mara.

THE MARA OF THE AGGREGATES

Here, 'aggregates' refers to the five contaminated aggregates of a person within samsara. These aggregates are
contaminated because they arise as a result of actions contaminated by delusions. The contaminated aggregates of
beings within samsara are the basis of their suffering. For
example, those who have the contaminated aggregates of a
human being experience the sufferings of a human, and
those who have the contaminated aggregates of a dog
experience the sufferings of a dog.

If we wish to gain liberation or full enlightenment we
need to completely abandon contaminated aggregates by
overcoming rebirth within samsara. Our contaminated
aggregates are therefore an obstacle to liberation as well as
the basis of our present suffering. For this reason they are
called a mara.

THE MARA OF THE LORD OF DEATH

The mara of the Lord of Death refers to ordinary uncontrolled death. Quite clearly, uncontrolled death can be a
very serious interruption to our progress towards liberation
and enlightenment. If we lose our wealth or possessions
there are methods we can use to replace them, but there is
no method to retrieve this life once death has robbed us of
it. Once this life is finished, the resources we have accumulated become completely useless to us. More seriously

though, death deprives us of the chance to complete our spiritual practice. Unless we have thoroughly purified our negative actions and gained firm control over our body, speech, and mind, we cannot be confident that we shall gain a fortunate rebirth after death. Instead we may plunge into a rebirth in the lower realms where spiritual practice is impossible and escape is very difficult.

DEVAPUTRA MARA

Although the previous three sources of interference are called maras, or demons, they are not animate beings. The Devaputra maras, on the other hand, are actual beings who interfere with our spiritual progress to liberation and enlightenment.

The most common mara of this type is Black Ishvara. This god abides in the land known as 'Land of Controlling Emanations', which is the highest state of existence within the desire realm. This god has limited, contaminated miracle powers, which make him very powerful compared with other beings in the desire realm. If we entrust ourself to Ishvara we may receive some temporary benefit in this life, such as an increase in our wealth and possessions; but Black Ishvara is the enemy of those seeking liberation, and interferes with our spiritual progress. For this reason he is sometimes known simply as 'Mara'.

When Buddha Shakyamuni was about to demonstrate the attainment of final enlightenment under the Bodhi Tree it was Mara and his entourage who tried to disturb him. Mara manifested visions of alluring, beautiful women to arouse desirous attachment, and rained down weapons to incite anger. However, none of these ploys succeeded. Buddha Shakyamuni overcame these interferences through the force of his meditative concentration on love.

Anyone who becomes completely free from these four maras attains full enlightenment and becomes a Buddha. In fact, because they have overcome, or conquered, the four maras, Buddhas are given the name 'Conqueror'. Hinayana Foe Destroyers have gained freedom from the gross levels of interference by the four maras, but only Buddhas have gained release from the most subtle levels of interference.

ILLUSTRATIONS OF THE PRACTICE OF THE SUTRA

There is no more powerful remedy for overcoming hindrances and interferences than the practice of the perfection of wisdom as revealed in the *Essence of Wisdom Sutra*. There are many instances of sincere practitioners of the perfection of wisdom using this Sutra to avert harm and hindrances.

There was once a time when the god Indra was in danger of losing his life because of an attack by the powerful forces of jealous demi-gods. Indra had previously received teachings from Buddha and knew that to kill the demi-gods would be a serious transgression of those teachings. Wishing therefore to overcome his attackers by a peaceful method, Indra contemplated the profound meaning of the *Essence of Wisdom Sutra* while reciting its words. Through the power of this contemplation and recitation the demi-gods ceased their attack; their anger subsided and their minds became peaceful and happy.

There are accounts of similar events taking place in Tibet. For example, there was once a very powerful practitioner of black magic called Kulo, who brought great harm and even death to a large number of people in the area of Tibet where he lived. Fortunately at that time there lived nearby a pure Dharma practitioner called Lama Ukarwa. This Lama could not bear to allow the suffering inflicted by the wicked Kulo to continue unopposed, so one day he confronted the magician in the presence of a great crowd of people and said to him: 'It is true that you are a very powerful man, but if you continue your evil actions you will certainly be reborn in one of the lower realms and there you will have to experience great suffering. Therefore it would be much better for you in the future if you gave up these harmful actions.'

However, Kulo, far from accepting this advice, became even more angry and uncontrolled. 'You are going to be the very next person I kill', he shouted. 'Before this week is over, you will be dead as a result of my magic.'

He declared this before the frightened crowd and then stormed off, his mind consumed by hatred. All the people were very saddened by this. They were quite sure that within a week Lama Ukarwa would be dead because no one could withstand Kulo's magic. However Ukarwa himself returned calmly to his home and began to practise a technique for averting harm that he had learned from a Kadampa master. This involved reciting and contemplating the *Essence of Wisdom Sutra*, which he did with great faith and concentration over the following days. Then, on the last day of the week, just as Kulo had predicted, there was a sudden death – but it was the magician himself and not Ukarwa who had died!

The people were amazed at this unexpected turn of events and thought that perhaps the Lama had also practised black magic during the week. They came to him and asked whether this was true. Ukarwa replied that he had not done anything to kill or even to harm the magician, explaining that he had no such power and certainly no such intention. He told them that he had practised a technique to avert hindrances, and as a result Kulo's magic had been neutralized. He suggested that perhaps Kulo's own evil powers had turned against him and caused his death. Ukarwa emphasized that he had had no intention to kill the magician.

Inspired by these events the people requested teachings on the *Essence of Wisdom Sutra* and also received instruction on how to avert dangers using the Sutra. Many of them received signs indicating that their practice was successful, and thus they gained protection from various hindrances.

As a result of occurrences such as this, the practices to avert hindrances using this Sutra became very popular in Tibet. There are many people who have direct personal experience of how effective these practices can be. For instance, in 1954, Shigatse, the second largest city in Tibet, was in great danger of being flooded. After many houses had been destroyed, the local people requested the monks of nearby Tashi Lhunpo monastery to help avert the disaster. The monks left their monastery and assembled facing the approaching flood waters. First they recited the *Essence of Wisdom Sutra*, and then they repeated the mantra of the perfection of wisdom many times, clapping their hands as indicated in the practice. As they did this, the waters receded and the danger was averted, to the great relief of the people of the city.

Many Tibetans have some experience of the great benefits of these practices. Very often if a family member becomes ill a Lama will be invited to their house to recite the Sutra and perform other rituals. I myself have participated in such practices and I have seen personally how effective they can be. Also, those who have attended many teachings given by Tibetan Lamas will know that it is the custom to recite the *Essence of Wisdom Sutra* before the start of the discourses in order to avert obstacles to the transmission and comprehension of the teachings.

As briefly mentioned above, at one point during the practice to avert hindrances we clap our hands together. The purpose of this is to remind us of emptiness. In many texts it is stated that it is easier to develop an understanding of emptiness through contemplating sound than through contemplating other external objects such as visual form. When we clap our hands we can think: 'Where is the sound? Is it on the right hand? On the left hand? Somewhere in between? Or perhaps somewhere else?' If we check like this, we cannot find the sound. Realizing that the sound cannot be found leads us to an understanding of emptiness.

An example of teaching emptiness using sound as the basis is found in the last chapters of the *Perfection of Wisdom Sutra in Eight Thousand Lines*. There a story is told about the great teacher Dharmodgata, who reveals the profound view of emptiness to the Bodhisattva Sadaprarudita by taking the sound of a lute as an example. It may be helpful to give a brief outline of this story.

Sadaprarudita was given this name, which means 'the one who is always crying', because he was filled with grief having searched unsuccessfully for a qualified Teacher who could reveal the perfection of wisdom. He would not give up his search, however, and asked everyone he met 'Where is the Teacher who can reveal to me the profound perfection of wisdom?'

One day, through the power of having purified the stains of previous non-virtuous actions, there appeared in the space before him a vision of a Buddha. The vision spoke to him, saying that he should travel east to a town called Gandhavati. There he would find the great Bodhisattva Dharmodgata, who would give teachings on the perfection of wisdom. The vision of the Buddha then vanished. Upon hearing these words Sadaprarudita was so joyful that he experienced a feeling of bliss similar to the blissful suppleness experienced by Yogis in deep meditation.

Sadaprarudita then reflected that he would like to bring a gift to Dharmodgata to express his respect and reverence for him. However, Sadaprarudita was poor and unable to buy even the smallest gift. Finally he thought: 'At the moment I am endowed with this human body of flesh and bone. If I do not make use of it now, when shall I be able to use it? If I sell portions of this body to others I shall be able to buy worthy offerings for my Teacher, Dharmodgata.' Filled with the strong determination to sell his own body to fulfil his wish to make offerings, he travelled to a nearby town and stood in the market place crying out 'Is there anyone here who would like to buy my body?' Despite his loud cries no one seemed to hear him. Greatly disappointed, Sadaprarudita went to one side and wept.

Thereupon, the chief of the gods, Indra, having seen what had happened, decided to test the resolve of Sadaprarudita. In the guise of a high-caste Brahmin he approached Sadaprarudita and said 'Normally I have no use for human flesh but, as it happens, today there is a special ceremony and I need a man's flesh, blood, and marrow. If you give these to me I shall pay you.'

Hearing this, Sadaprarudita was overjoyed. He immediately cut some flesh from his right thigh and drew to one side to smash his bone. The daughter of a local merchant living nearby witnessed this astonishing scene. Rushing outside, she asked Sadaprarudita why he was inflicting such treatment upon himself. The Bodhisattva explained that he was selling his flesh to buy offerings so that he could honour the great Bodhisattva, Dharmodgata. The merchant's daughter then asked him why he wished to honour Dharmodgata and what benefits he hoped to receive. Sadaprarudita replied: 'Dharmodgata will explain to me the perfection of wisdom and skilful means. Through training in these I shall attain great enlightenment and share the precious Dharma with all living beings.' When he explained the excellent qualities of Buddhahood, the young woman developed great respect for the Three Jewels. She implored Sadaprarudita not to harm himself further, and declared 'I will give you whatever you require to honour Dharmodgata and I will come with you to him.'

Indra then threw off his disguise and stood before Sadaprarudita in his normal form. He proclaimed to the Bodhisattva: 'All the Buddhas of the past attained enlightenment through having just such a desire for Dharma as you have. I have no need of your flesh – I came here only to test you. Now choose what you will, and I will give it to you.'

Sadaprarudita answered 'Give me the supreme qualities of a Buddha!' Indra explained that such a request lay within the province of the Buddhas alone; it was not within his power to grant. Sadaprarudita told Indra that he required no other wish to be granted, and explained that he was able to heal his mutilated body through his special powers of declaring the truth. By these means his body was restored to its former whole state.

The story continues with an account of how Sadaprarudita finally met with Dharmodgata and made offerings to him. One of the first questions Sadaprarudita asked concerned the visions of the Buddha who had appeared and spoken to him. He asked Dharmodgata 'Where did this Buddha come from and where did he go to?'

Dharmodgata replied 'Buddhas do not come from anywhere, nor do they go anywhere. Since Buddhas lack inherent existence they are completely empty.' It was then that Dharmodgata used the example of the sound of a lute to illustrate his point. He asked Sadaprarudita: 'Where does the sound of a lute come from and where does it go? Does it come from the strings, from within the lute, from the fingers of the player, from his effort to play, or from elsewhere? And when the sound has stopped, where does it go?'

In this way Dharmodgata explained that although Buddhas are empty of inherent existence they appear in dependence upon many causes and conditions, and when these causes and conditions cease, Buddhas no longer appear. In this respect, Buddhas are like the sound of a lute. If we try to find the sound upon the strings of the lute, or upon the fingers of the player and so forth, we are unable to find it. This is because the sound is empty of inherent existence. Nevertheless, when all the appropriate causes and conditions are assembled the sound of a lute will be produced, and when those causes and conditions cease the sound stops.

After Dharmodgata's explanation of the non-coming and non-going of Buddhas, using the illustration of the sound of a lute, the whole earth shook and many thousands of beings gained profound realizations of emptiness. Finally, through Dharmodgata's teachings on the perfection of wisdom Sadaprarudita attained extraordinary concentrations on emptiness, and many miracle powers.

The reason for recounting this story here is to illustrate that sound can be a very helpful basis for realizing emptiness. Thus, during the practice for averting hindrances that is explained next, we clap our hands four times to strengthen our recollection of emptiness. The story of Sadaprarudita also illustrates that in the past sincere practitioners were prepared to make determined efforts and undergo great hardships in order to receive teachings on the perfection of wisdom. They were happy to do this because they understood the great benefits of achieving and completing the perfection of wisdom.

Prajnaparamita

THE ACTUAL PRACTICE TO OVERCOME HINDRANCES

I will now describe a practice involving the recitation and contemplation of the *Essence of Wisdom Sutra* that can be used to avert or overcome hindrances and obstacles. The method can be used to overcome both the hindrances that afflict oneself and those afflicting others. The practice can also be directed towards overcoming both internal and external obstacles. The extent to which we are successful in overcoming obstacles through this practice, however, depends on the strength of our faith.

The text of this practice is as follows:

Going for refuge

I and all sentient beings, until we achieve enlightenment,
Go for refuge to Buddha, Dharma, and Sangha.   (3x)

Generating bodhichitta

Through the virtues I collect by giving and other
      perfections,
May I become a Buddha for the benefit of all.   (3x)

Preliminaries

NAMO Guru, Teacher, Blessed One, and the Great
      Mother Prajnaparamita,
Surrounded by your Sons, the Buddhas of the ten
      directions and all Bodhisattvas;
I prostrate to this assembly, make offerings, and go
      for refuge,
Please empower me with your blessings.   (3x)

Reciting the *Essence of Wisdom Sutra*

At this point we recite the complete Essence of Wisdom
Sutra.

Reciting the mantra

TAYATHA OM GATE GATE PARAGATE PARASAMGATE
    BODHI SÖHA   (3x, 7x, etc.)

Requests to overcome hindrances

Great Mother Prajnaparamita, and all the Buddhas
and Bodhisattvas of the ten directions, through the
power of your blessings may these true words of mine
be achieved. Just as before, when by contemplating
the profound meaning of the perfection of wisdom
and reciting its words, Indra overcame all the harm
of maras, non-humans, and so forth, in the same
way, by my contemplating the profound meaning of
the perfection of wisdom and reciting its words,

May all the harm of maras, non-humans,
    and so forth be overcome.   (*clap*)
May they become non-existent.   (*clap*)
May they be pacified.   (*clap*)
May they be thoroughly pacified.   (*clap*)

Dedication and prayer

May all kinds of interferences, diseases, and
    possessing spirits be pacified.

May I be separated from unfavourable conditions
And may I achieve favourable conditions and
   everything excellent.
Through this fortune may there be at this time
   happiness and health.

We begin this practice by visualizing the objects of refuge. In the space in front of us we visualize an extensive jewelled throne supported by eight snow lions. In the centre of this throne is a lotus flower, upon which is a moon seat (a circular cushion of white light) and a sun seat (a circular cushion of yellow light). Seated on the sun seat is the founder of the teachings, Buddha Shakyamuni, in his usual posture – his left hand rests in his lap holding a bowl, his right hand is in the earth-touching mudra, and his legs are crossed in the vajra posture. His body has the nature of golden light and he wears the robes of a fully ordained monk.

At Buddha Shakyamuni's heart we visualize another lotus, moon, and sun seat. Upon this is seated the Great Mother Prajnaparamita, who is the embodiment of the Wisdom Truth Body of all the Buddhas. She has a body of golden light with one face and four arms. Her first right hand holds a golden vajra with nine prongs at each end, and her first left hand holds the *Perfection of Wisdom Sutra*. Her remaining two hands rest in her lap in the mudra of meditative equipoise. She is seated in the vajra posture, adorned with precious jewels and ornaments, and she wears beautiful garments of thin, heavenly material. We visualize Buddha Shakyamuni and the Great Mother as real, living beings – not lifeless like paintings or statues.

On the extensive throne, surrounding the two principal objects of refuge, are all the Buddhas and Bodhisattvas of the ten directions. In this way we visualize a vast assembly of refuge objects in the space before us. Without forgetting this visualization, we begin reciting the practice.

First we recite three times the verses of going for refuge and generating bodhichitta. While we recite the first verse we remember the fears that face ourself and others, and with great faith go for refuge to the Three Jewels. While we recite the second verse we generate bodhichitta, the mind wishing to attain Buddhahood for the benefit of all living beings.

We then recite the third verse three times. During this recitation we focus our mind on the visualized objects of refuge. We prostrate to them, make offerings, and go for refuge. Finally we request their blessings. Here, when making prostrations, it is sufficient to place our hands together at our heart and generate a mind of respect and faith. We can make actual offerings of fresh water, flowers, and so forth, or just visualize beautiful offerings being made.

Having completed these preliminaries we recite the text of the *Essence of Wisdom Sutra*. During this recitation we should maintain our faith and devotion towards the assembly of refuge objects, and also contemplate the meaning of the Sutra.

When we have finished reciting the Sutra we turn our attention to the heart of Prajnaparamita. There, standing at the centre of a white moon cushion, a blue letter HUM, marked by a letter AH, appears. We can visualize this as the Tibetan or Sanskrit letter, or as the English syllable.

Surrounding the letter HUM, around the edge of the moon cushion, stand the letters of the perfection of wisdom mantra in a clockwise direction. The letters of the mantra are made of golden light but have the nature of the wisdom of Prajnaparamita herself. As we concentrate on these letters we remember the profound meaning of emptiness and recite the mantra. While reciting the mantra of the perfection of wisdom we contemplate that we and all that offends and harms us are empty of inherent existence. We recite the mantra as many times as is comfortable.

After the mantra recitation we make requests to avert hindrances. While we recite the requesting verses we think about the harms and hindrances that we wish to overcome. When we reach the point where we recite:

> May all the harm of maras, non-humans, and so
>   forth be overcome

we clap our hands and imagine that the harms and hindrances gather together into emptiness. Then, when we recite:

> May they become non-existent

we clap again and imagine that they dissolve into emptiness. When we recite:

> May they be pacified

we clap and imagine that they cease completely in emptiness. Finally, when we recite:

> May they be thoroughly pacified

we clap for the fourth time and think that none of the harms and hindrances can ever arise again. As explained earlier, we clap our hands each time to remember emptiness. There are other similar practices in which we clap our hands three or nine times. Each system has its own significance and suitability.

We then meditate on emptiness. We can think that we, all that harms us, and the harm itself are all empty of inherent existence. We try to generate this realization and maintain it as well as we can. After the meditation on emptiness we recite the remaining dedication verse.

If we wish to use this practice to overcome the four maras that afflict ourself and others, there is a particular visualization that we can do during the part of the practice where we make requests to avert hindrances. We recall the harm and suffering experienced by all living beings as a result of the mara of the delusions and the other maras, and, using this as a basis, we generate the mind of great compassion and a strong wish to free all living beings from the four maras.

For the purpose of this practice we visualize the four maras in physical form. We visualize the mara of the delusions as a host of yellow human beings riding yellow horses. Each rider holds a metal sword in his right hand and a noose in his left. It is important to remember that in essence these horsemen are delusions – the delusions are merely appearing in this aspect. Because the delusions that afflict living beings are beyond measure, we visualize these horsemen filling the whole of space.

The visualizations of the other three maras are very similar, differing only in the colour of the horses and riders and the weapons carried. In the case of the mara of the aggregates, the horses and riders are red, and the riders carry a spear and noose. The mara of the Lord of Death appears as black horsemen upon black horses, holding a wooden sword and a noose. Lastly, we visualize the Devaputra maras as white horsemen upon white horses, holding a white flower and a noose.

When we clap our hands the first time we imagine that all the yellow horsemen, who in essence are delusions, gather and dissolve into emptiness, become non-existent, and will never arise again, like a rainbow dissolving into the sky without leaving a trace. We then think that we have accomplished our wish to free all living beings from delusions. Then, when we clap our hands the second time we imagine that the red horsemen, who in essence are the contaminated aggregates of all sentient beings, gather and dissolve into emptiness, become non-existent, and will never arise again. Similarly, when we clap our hands the third time we destroy the black horsemen who are the mara of the Lord of Death; and when we clap our hands the fourth time we destroy the white horsemen who are the Devaputra maras. When we have completed this practice we think 'I have now freed all living beings from the four maras!' and we try to generate a feeling of great joy.

This practice is an excellent method for developing great compassion and bodhichitta, as well as for developing wisdom realizing emptiness. When we eventually attain Buddhahood through completing the spiritual paths of method and wisdom we shall actually have the ability to help others overcome the four maras. The practice described here takes the future result, Buddhahood, and uses it in the path right now. By imagining that we already have abilities that we wish to gain in the future, we create the cause to attain them more quickly.

Finally, it should be mentioned that these practices to avert hindrances can be done in either a peaceful or a wrathful manner. The method described here is the peaceful method. Those who have received an empowerment into Highest Yoga Tantra may do these practices in a powerful, wrathful manner. However, whichever way we do these practices, we should be mindful of the underlying meaning of what we are doing. Simply clapping our hands has no great meaning. To attain true freedom from obstacles and to accomplish full awakening to Buddhahood it is necessary to gain experience of the actual perfection of wisdom.

Dedication

Through the force of composing this commentary I send forth the prayer that all fighting among the nations of this planet may immediately come to an end. May the dangers afflicting humankind be pacified quickly. May every living being without exception remain forever in peace. May the pure teachings of Sutra and Secret Mantra flourish throughout the world so that all may reach the ultimate peace and happiness of full enlightenment.

Appendix I
The Root Text:
Essence of Wisdom Sutra

The Root Text:
Essence of Wisdom Sutra

Essence of the perfection of wisdom, the Blessed Mother

Bhagavatiprajnaparamitahrdaya

bCom ldan 'das ma shes rab kyi pha rol tu phyin p'ai snying po
(Chom dän dä ma she rab kyi pa röl tu jin pai nying po)

Homage to the perfection of wisdom, the Blessed Mother.

Thus I have heard. At one time the Blessed One was dwelling in Rajagriha on Massed Vultures Mountain together with a great assembly of monks and a great assembly of Bodhisattvas. At that time the Blessed One was absorbed in the concentration of the countless aspects of phenomena, called 'Profound Illumination'.

At that time also the Superior Avalokiteshvara, the Bodhisattva, the Great Being, was looking perfectly at the practice of the profound perfection of wisdom, looking perfectly at the emptiness of inherent existence also of the five aggregates.

Then, through the power of Buddha, the Venerable Shariputra said to the Superior Avalokiteshvara, the Bodhisattva, the Great Being, 'How should a Son of the lineage train who wishes to engage in the practice of the profound perfection of wisdom?'

Thus he spoke, and the Superior Avalokiteshvara, the Bodhisattva, the Great Being, replied to the Venerable Shariputra as follows:

'Shariputra, whatever Son or Daughter of the lineage wishes to engage in the practice of the profound perfection of wisdom should look perfectly like this: subsequently looking perfectly and correctly at the emptiness of inherent existence also of the five aggregates.

'Form is empty; emptiness is form. Emptiness is not other than form; form also is not other than emptiness. Likewise, feeling, discrimination, compositional factors, and consciousness are empty.

'Shariputra, like this all phenomena are merely empty, having no characteristics. They are not produced and do not cease. They have no defilement and no separation from defilement. They have no decrease and no increase.

'Therefore, Shariputra, in emptiness there is no form, no feeling, no discrimination, no compositional factors, no consciousness. There is no eye, no ear, no nose, no tongue, no body, no mentality; no form, no sound, no smell, no taste, no tactile object, no phenomenon. There is no eye element and so forth up to no mentality element and also up to no element of mental consciousness. There is no ignorance and no exhaustion of ignorance and so forth up to no ageing and death and no exhaustion of ageing and death. Likewise, there is no suffering, origin, cessation, or path; no exalted awareness, no attainment, and also no non-attainment.

'Therefore, Shariputra, because there is no attainment, Bodhisattvas rely upon and abide in the perfection of wisdom; their minds have no obstructions and no fear. Passing utterly beyond perversity, they attain the final nirvana. Also all the Buddhas who reside perfectly in the three times, having relied upon the perfection of wisdom, became manifest and complete Buddhas in the state of unsurpassed, perfect, and complete enlightenment.

'Therefore, the mantra of the perfection of wisdom, the mantra of great knowledge, the unsurpassed mantra, the equal-to-the-unequalled mantra, the mantra that thoroughly pacifies all suffering, since it is not false, should be known as the truth. The mantra of the perfection of wisdom is proclaimed:

TAYATHA OM GATE GATE PARAGATE PARASAMGATE BODHI
    SÖHA

'Shariputra, a Bodhisattva, a Great Being, should train in the profound perfection of wisdom like this.'

Then the Blessed One arose from that concentration and said to the Superior Avalokiteshvara, the Bodhisattva, the Great Being, that he had spoken well: 'Good, good, O Son of the lineage. It is like that. Since it is like that, just as you have revealed, in that way the profound perfection of wisdom should be practised, and the Tathagatas will also rejoice.'

When the Blessed One had said this, the Venerable Shariputra, the Superior Avalokiteshvara, the Bodhisattva, the Great Being, and that entire circle of disciples as well as the worldly beings – gods, humans, demi-gods, and spirits – were delighted and highly praised what had been spoken by the Blessed One.

Appendix II
The Condensed Meaning
of the Commentary

The Condensed Meaning
of the Commentary

The commentary to the *Essence of Wisdom Sutra* has four parts:

1 The meaning of the title
2 The homage of the translators
3 An explanation of the main body of the Sutra
4 Conclusion

An explanation of the main body of the Sutra has two parts:

1 An explanation of the background to the Sutra
2 An explanation of the actual Sutra

An explanation of the background to the Sutra has two parts:

1 The common explanation of the background to the Sutra
2 The uncommon explanation of the background to the Sutra

An explanation of the actual Sutra has four parts:

1 The question of Shariputra
2 The answers by Avalokiteshvara
3 The approval of the answers by Buddha
4 The followers are pleased and take the teachings
   to heart

The answers by Avalokiteshvara has three parts:

1 The answer intended for those with minds of
   lower faculties
2 The answer intended for those with minds of
   higher faculties
3 The exhortation to practise the perfection of
   wisdom

The answer intended for those with minds of lower faculties
has five parts:

1 A brief explanation of how to practise the
   perfection of wisdom on the paths of accumulation
   and preparation
2 An extensive explanation of how to practise the
   perfection of wisdom on the paths of accumulation
   and preparation
3 An explanation of how to practise the perfection of
   wisdom on the path of seeing
4 An explanation of how to practise the perfection of
   wisdom on the path of meditation
5 An explanation of how to attain the Path of No
   More Learning

An extensive explanation of how to practise the perfection of wisdom on the paths of accumulation and preparation has two parts:

1 The meditation on the four profundities of the aggregate of form
2 The meditation on the four profundities of the aggregates of feeling and so forth

The meditation on the four profundities of the aggregate of form has four parts:

1 The meditation on the first profundity of the aggregate of form
2 The meditation on the second profundity of the aggregate of form
3 The meditation on the third profundity of the aggregate of form
4 The meditation on the fourth profundity of the aggregate of form

Appendix III
Liberating Prayer

PRAISE TO BUDDHA SHAKYAMUNI

Liberating Prayer

O Blessed One, Shakyamuni Buddha,
Precious treasury of compassion,
Bestower of supreme inner peace,

You, who love all beings without exception,
Are the source of happiness and goodness;
And you guide us to the liberating path.

Your body is a wishfulfilling jewel,
Your speech is supreme, purifying nectar,
And your mind is a refuge for all living beings.

With folded hands I turn to you,
Supreme unchanging friend,
I request from the depths of my heart:

Please give me the light of your wisdom
To dispel the darkness of my mind
And to heal my mental continuum.

Please nourish me with your goodness,
That I in turn may nourish all beings
With an unceasing banquet of delight.

Through your compassionate intention,
Your blessings and virtuous deeds,
And my strong wish to rely upon you,

May all suffering quickly cease
And all happiness and joy be fulfilled;
And may holy Dharma flourish for evermore.

Colophon: This prayer was composed by
Geshe Kelsang Gyatso Rinpoche.

Glossary

Atisha (AD 982-1054) A famous Indian Buddhist scholar and meditation master. He was Abbot of the great Buddhist monastery of Vikramashila at a time when Mahayana Buddhism was flourishing in India. He was later invited to Tibet and his arrival there led to the re-establishment of Buddhism in Tibet. He is the author of the first text on the stages of the path, *Lamp for the Path*. His tradition later became known as the 'Kadampa Tradition'. See *Joyful Path of Good Fortune*.

Bodhichitta Sanskrit word for 'mind of enlightenment'. 'Bodhi' means 'enlightenment', and 'chitta' means 'mind'. There are two types of bodhichitta – conventional bodhichitta and ultimate bodhichitta. Generally speaking, the term 'bodhichitta' refers to conventional bodhichitta, which is a primary mind motivated by great compassion that spontaneously seeks enlightenment to benefit all living beings. Conventional bodhichitta is of two types: aspiring bodhichitta and engaging bodhichitta. Ultimate bodhichitta is a wisdom motivated by conventional bodhichitta that directly realizes emptiness, the ultimate nature of phenomena. See *Joyful Path of Good Fortune*, *Meaningful to Behold*, and *Universal Compassion*.

Bodhisattva A person who has generated spontaneous bodhichitta but who has not yet become a Buddha. From the moment a practitioner generates a non-artificial, or spontaneous, bodhichitta he or she becomes a Bodhisattva and enters the first Mahayana path, the path of accumulation. An ordinary Bodhisattva is one who has not realized emptiness directly, and a Superior Bodhisattva is one who has attained a direct realization of emptiness. See *Joyful Path of Good Fortune* and *Meaningful to Behold*.

Brahma A worldly god (Skt. deva). See *Ocean of Nectar*.

Buddha Shakyamuni The fourth of one thousand founding Buddhas who are to appear in this world during this Fortunate Aeon. See *Introduction to Buddhism*.

Chandrakirti A great Indian Buddhist scholar and meditation master who composed, among many other books, the well-known *Guide to the Middle Way*, in which he clearly presents the view of the Madhyamika-Prasangika school according to Buddha's teachings given in the *Perfection of Wisdom Sutras*. See *Ocean of Nectar*.

Conceptual mind A thought that apprehends its object through a generic image. See *Understanding the Mind*.

Cyclic existence See *Samsara*.

Deluded doubt A two-pointedness of mind that interferes with the attainment of liberation or enlightenment. See *Understanding the Mind*.

Dependent-related ignorance See *Ignorance*.

Dependent-related phenomenon Any phenomenon that exists in dependence upon other phenomena. All phenomena are dependent-related because all phenomena depend upon their parts. Sometimes 'dependent-related' (Tib. ten drel) is distinguished from 'dependent arising' (Tib. ten jung), with the latter meaning arising in dependence upon causes and conditions. However, the two terms are often used interchangeably. See *Joyful Path of Good Fortune* and *Ocean of Nectar*.

Desire realm The environment of hell beings, hungry ghosts, animals, humans, demi-gods, and the gods who enjoy the five objects of desire.

Dharma Buddha's teachings and the inner realizations that are attained in dependence upon them. 'Dharma' means 'protection'. By practising Buddha's teachings we protect ourself from suffering and problems.

Direct perceiver (Tib. ngön sum) A cognizer that apprehends its manifest object. According to the lower Buddhist schools a direct perceiver is necessarily non-conceptual, but according to the Madhyamika-Prasangikas direct perceivers include the subsequent moments of an inferential cognizer, which are conceptual minds. See *Understanding the Mind*.

Direct valid cognizer A non-deceptive cognizer that apprehends its manifest object. See *Understanding the Mind*.

Doubt A mental factor that wavers with respect to its object. See *Understanding the Mind*.

Eight Great Sons The eight principal Mahayana disciples of Buddha Shakyamuni: Avalokiteshvara, Manjushri, Vajrapani, Maitreya, Samantabhadra, Ksitigarbha, Sarvanivaranaviskambini, and Akashagarbha. At the time of Buddha they appeared in the aspect of Bodhisattvas, demonstrating the correct manner of practising the Mahayana paths and helping to spread Buddha's teachings extensively for the benefit of others.

Element (Tib. kham) The nature of any phenomenon. All phenomena hold their own natures, which are all included within the eighteen elements. See also *Four elements*. See *Ocean of Nectar*.

Emanation Body (Skt. Nirmanakaya) A Buddha's Form Body that can be perceived by ordinary beings. In general, Buddhas manifest in many different forms. The aspect of some of these emanations is mundane, even though in essence they are Buddhas. Also, a Buddha may manifest as a person with Hinayana realizations or as a Bodhisattva. An emanation who performs the twelve principal deeds, such as Buddha Shakyamuni, is called a 'Supreme Emanation Body'. From the point of view of external aspect such an emanation is supreme, but from the point of view of nature all beings emanated by a Buddha, however mundane in aspect, are supreme beings. Therefore we should not infer from the name 'Supreme Emanation Body' that there are higher and lower emanations of Buddha. In essence, all Buddha's emanations are fully enlightened beings. See *Tantric Grounds and Paths*.

Empowerment A special potential power to attain any of the four Buddha bodies that is received by a Tantric practitioner from his or her Guru, or from other holy beings, by means of Tantric ritual. It is the gateway to the Vajrayana. See *Tantric Grounds and Paths*.

Enjoyment Body (Skt. Sambhogakaya) A Buddha's subtle Form Body that can be perceived only by Mahayana Superiors. See *Tantric Grounds and Paths*.

Foe Destroyer (Skt. Arhat) A practitioner who has abandoned all delusions and their seeds by training on the spiritual paths, and who will never again be born in samsara. In this context the term 'Foe' refers to the delusions.

Form realm The environment of the gods who possess form.

Formless realm The environment of the gods who do not possess form.

Fortunate Aeon The name given to this world age. It is so called because one thousand founding Buddhas will appear during this aeon. Buddha Shakyamuni was the fourth and Buddha Maitreya will be the fifth. An aeon in which no Buddhas appear is called a 'Dark Aeon'.

Four classes of Tantra Buddha taught four classes of Tantra: Action (Skt. Kriya) Tantra, Performance (Skt. Charya) Tantra, Yoga Tantra, and Highest Yoga (Skt. Anuttarayoga) Tantra. See *Tantric Grounds and Paths*.

Four elements (Tib. jung wa) Earth, water, fire, and wind. There are four inner elements (those that are conjoined with the continuum of a person), and four outer elements (those that are not conjoined with the continuum of a person). There are different ways in which matter can be considered to be composed of parts or ingredients. Among scientists, matter is presently considered to be composed of atomic elements, these elements being classified in terms of nuclear charge. We can also consider matter to be composed of the elements of earth, water, fire, and wind. These four elements are not the same as the earth of a field, the water of a river, and so forth. Rather, the elements of earth, water, fire, and wind in broad terms are the properties of solidity, liquidity, heat, and movement respectively. All matter can be said to be composed of a combination of these elements.

Four opponent powers Four powers that are essential for successful purification: the power of reliance, the power of regret, the power of the opponent force, and the power of promise. See *Joyful Path of Good Fortune*, *The Bodhisattva Vow*, and *Meaningful to Behold*.

Generic image The appearing object of a conceptual mind. The conceptual mind mistakes the generic image for the object itself. For example, if we think about our mother, an image of our mother appears to our conceptual mind, and it seems to that mind as if our mother herself is appearing. However, the object that principally appears to that mind is the generic image of our mother. This generic image appears to our mind through the mental exclusion of all objects that are not our mother. It is therefore the appearance of a non-non-mother. As such, like all generic images, it is a permanent phenomenon, whereas our mother herself is impermanent. See *Understanding the Mind*.

Geshe A title given by the Kadampa Monasteries to accomplished Buddhist scholars. Contracted form of 'ge wai she nyen', literally meaning 'virtuous friend'.

Great compassion A mind wishing to protect all sentient beings from suffering. See *Eight Steps to Happiness*, *Universal Compassion*, and *Ocean of Nectar*.

Great seal (Skt. Mahamudra) According to Sutra this refers to the profound view of emptiness. Since emptiness is the nature of all phenomena it is called a 'seal', and since a direct realization of emptiness enables us to accomplish the great purpose – complete liberation from the sufferings of samsara – it is also called 'great'. According to Secret Mantra, great seal is the union of spontaneous great bliss and emptiness. See *Great Treasury of Merit* and *Clear Light of Bliss*.

Ground/Spiritual ground A clear realization that acts as the foundation of many good qualities. A clear realization is a realization held by spontaneous renunciation or bodhichitta. The ten grounds are the realizations of Superior Bodhisattvas. They are: Very Joyful, Stainless, Luminous, Radiant, Difficult to Overcome, Approaching, Gone Afar, Immovable, Good Intelligence, and Cloud of Dharma. See *Ocean of Nectar* and *Tantric Grounds and Paths*.

Hearer One of two types of Hinayana practitioner. Both Hearers and Solitary Conquerors are Hinayanists, but they differ in their motivation, behaviour, merit, and wisdom. In all these respects Solitary Conquerors are superior to Hearers. See *Ocean of Nectar*.

Hidden object An object whose initial realization by a valid cognizer depends upon correct logical reasons. See *Understanding the Mind*.

Hinayana Sanskrit word for 'Lesser Vehicle'. The Hinayana goal is to attain merely one's own liberation from suffering by completely abandoning delusions. See *Joyful Path of Good Fortune*.

Ignorance A mental factor that is confused about the ultimate nature of phenomena. Although all ignorance is dependent-related, not all ignorance is the dependent-related ignorance of the twelve links. A mind of self-grasping that does not motivate a person to create a compositional action is ignorance and is dependent-related, but it is not dependent-related ignorance.

Impermanent phenomenon Phenomena are either permanent or impermanent. 'Impermanent' means 'momentary', thus an impermanent phenomenon is a phenomenon that is produced and disintegrates within a moment. Synonyms of impermanent phenomenon are 'functioning thing' and 'product'.

Imprint There are two types of imprint: imprints of actions and imprints of delusions. Every action we perform leaves an imprint on the mental consciousness, and these imprints are karmic potentialities to experience certain effects in the future. The imprints left by delusions remain even after the delusions themselves have been abandoned, rather as the smell of garlic lingers in a container after the garlic has been removed. Imprints of delusions are obstructions to omniscience, and are completely abandoned only by Buddhas.

Indra A worldly god (Skt. deva).

Inferential cognizer A completely reliable cognizer whose object is realized in direct dependence upon a conclusive reason. The Tibetan word for 'subsequently' is 'je su', and the Tibetan word for 'inferential cognizer' is 'je pag'. See *Understanding the Mind*.

Je Phabongkhapa (AD 1878-1941) A great Tibetan Lama who was an emanation of Heruka. Phabongkha Rinpoche was the holder of many lineages of Sutra and Secret Mantra. He was the root Guru of Yongdzin Trijang Dorjechang (Trijang Rinpoche).

Je Tsongkhapa (AD 1357-1419) An emanation of the Wisdom Buddha Manjushri, whose appearance in fourteenth-century Tibet as a monk and the holder of the lineage of pure view and pure deeds was prophesied by Buddha. He spread a very pure Buddhadharma throughout Tibet, showing how to combine the practices of Sutra and Tantra, and how to practise pure Dharma during degenerate times. His tradition later became known as the 'Gelug', or 'Ganden Tradition'. See *Heart Jewel* and *Great Treasury of Merit*.

Kadampa A Tibetan word in which 'Ka' means 'word' and refers to all Buddha's teachings, 'dam' refers to Atisha's special Lamrim instructions known as the 'stages of the path to enlightenment', and 'pa' refers to a follower of Kadampa Buddhism who integrates all the teachings of Buddha that they know into their Lamrim practice. See also *Kadampa Buddhism*.

Kadampa Buddhism A Mahayana Buddhist school founded by the great Indian Buddhist Master Atisha (AD 982-1054). See also *Kadampa*.

Karma Sanskrit word referring to actions. Through the force of intention we perform actions with our body, speech, and mind, and all of these actions produce effects. The effect of virtuous actions is happiness and the effect of negative actions is suffering. See *Joyful Path of Good Fortune*.

Lama Tibetan word for 'Spiritual Guide' (Skt. Guru).

Lineage A line of instruction that has been passed down from Spiritual Guide to disciple, with each Spiritual Guide in the line having gained personal experience of the instruction before passing it on to others.

Mahamudra See *Great seal*.

Mahayana Sanskrit word for 'Great Vehicle', the spiritual path to great enlightenment. The Mahayana goal is to attain Buddhahood for the benefit of all sentient beings by completely abandoning delusions and their imprints. See *Joyful Path of Good Fortune* and *Meaningful to Behold*.

Manifest object An object whose initial realization by a valid cognizer does not depend upon logical reasons. See *Understanding the Mind*.

Meditation Meditation is a mind that concentrates on a virtuous object, and is a mental action that is the main cause of mental peace. There are two types of meditation – analytical meditation and placement meditation. When we use our imagination, mindfulness, and powers of reasoning to find our object of meditation, this is analytical meditation. When we find our object and hold it single-pointedly, this is placement meditation. There are different types of object. Some, such as impermanence or emptiness, are objects apprehended by the mind. Others, such as love, compassion, and renunciation, are actual states of mind. We engage in analytical meditation until the specific object that we seek appears clearly to our mind, or until the particular state of mind that we wish to generate arises. This object or state of mind is our object of placement meditation. See *The Meditation Handbook*.

Meditative equipoise Single-pointed concentration on a virtuous object such as emptiness. See *Ocean of Nectar*.

Mental factor A cognizer that principally apprehends a particular attribute of an object. There are fifty-one specific mental factors. Each moment of mind comprises a primary mind and various mental factors. See *Understanding the Mind*.

Method Any spiritual path that functions to ripen our Buddha lineage. Training in renunciation, compassion, and bodhichitta are examples of method practices.

Migrators Beings within samsara who migrate from one uncontrolled birth to another.

Mind That which is clarity and cognizes. Mind is clarity because it always lacks form and because it possesses the actual power to perceive objects. Mind cognizes because its function is to know or perceive objects. See *Clear Light of Bliss* and *Understanding the Mind*.

Mistaken mind A mind that is mistaken with respect to its appearing object. Although all minds of ordinary beings are mistaken, they are not necessarily wrong. A wrong mind is a mind that is mistaken with respect to its engaged object. Thus our eye awareness perceiving this page is a mistaken mind because the page appears as inherently existent, but it is a correct mind because it correctly apprehends the page as a page. See *Understanding the Mind*.

Naga A non-human being not normally visible to humans. Their upper half is said to be human, their lower half serpent. Nagas usually live in the oceans of the world but they sometimes inhabit land in the region of rocks and trees. They are very powerful, some being benevolent and some malevolent. Many diseases, known as 'naga diseases', are caused by nagas, and can only be cured through performing certain naga rituals.

NAMO A Sanskrit word of homage and respect.

Negative phenomenon An object that is realized by means of the explicit elimination of a negated object. Emptiness is an example of a negative phenomenon because it is realized by a mind that directly negates inherent existence, which is its negated object. There are two types of negative phenomenon: affirming negatives and non-affirming negatives. See also *Non-affirming negative*. See *Ocean of Nectar*.

Non-affirming negative A negative phenomenon that does not imply another affirmative phenomenon. See also *Negative phenomenon*.

Non-conceptual mind A cognizer to which its object appears clearly without being mixed with a generic image. See *Understanding the Mind*.

Non-fabricated bodhichitta See *Spontaneous bodhichitta*.

Ordinary being Anyone who has not realized emptiness directly.

Permanent phenomenon A phenomenon that does not disintegrate moment by moment.

Primary mind A cognizer that principally apprehends the mere entity of an object. Synonymous with consciousness. There are six primary minds: eye consciousness, ear consciousness, nose consciousness, tongue consciousness, body consciousness, and mental consciousness. Each moment of mind comprises a primary mind and various mental factors. A primary mind and its accompanying mental factors are the same entity but have different functions. See *Understanding the Mind*.

Pure Land A pure environment in which there are no true sufferings. There are many Pure Lands. For example, Tushita is the Pure Land of Buddha Maitreya; Sukhavati is the Pure Land of Buddha Amitabha; and Dakini Land, or Keajra, is the Pure Land of Buddha Vajrayogini. See *Living Meaningfully, Dying Joyfully*.

Refuge Actual protection. To go for refuge to Buddha, Dharma, and Sangha means to have faith in these Three Jewels and to rely upon them for protection from all fears and suffering. See *Joyful Path of Good Fortune*.

Samsara This can be understood in two ways – as uninterrupted rebirth without freedom or control, or as the aggregates of a being who has taken such a rebirth. Samsara is characterized by suffering and dissatisfaction. There are six realms of samsara. Listed in ascending order according to the type of karma that causes rebirth in them, they are the realms of the hell beings, hungry ghosts, animals, humans, demi-gods, and gods. The first three are lower realms or unhappy migrations, and the second three are higher realms or happy migrations. See *Joyful Path of Good Fortune*.

Schools of Buddhist tenets Four philosophical views taught by Buddha according to the inclinations and dispositions of disciples. They are the Vaibashika, Sautrantika, Chittamatra, and Madhyamika schools. They are studied in sequence, the lower tenets being the means by which the higher ones are understood. The first two are Hinayana schools and the second two are Mahayana schools. See *Meaningful to Behold* and *Ocean of Nectar*.

Secret Mantra Synonymous with Tantra. Secret Mantra teachings are distinguished from Sutra teachings in that they reveal methods for training the mind by bringing the future result, or Buddhahood, into the present path. Secret Mantra is the supreme path to full enlightenment. The term 'Mantra' indicates that it is Buddha's special instruction for protecting our mind from ordinary appearances and conceptions. Practitioners of Secret Mantra overcome ordinary appearances and conceptions by visualizing their body, environment, enjoyments, and deeds as those of a Buddha. The term 'Secret' indicates that the practices are to be done in private, and that they can be practised only by those who have received a Tantric empowerment. See also *Four classes of Tantra*. See *Tantric Grounds and Paths*.

Seed of delusion The seed of a delusion is the potentiality for that delusion to arise; it is the substantial cause of the delusion. Until we have finally abandoned a delusion, the seed of that delusion will remain within our mind, even when the delusion itself is not manifest. Seeds of delusion can be eradicated only by the wisdom directly realizing emptiness. See *Understanding the Mind*.

Self-cherishing A mental attitude that considers oneself to be supremely important and precious. It is regarded as a principal object to be abandoned by Bodhisattvas. See *Eight Steps to Happiness* and *Meaningful to Behold*.

Sentient being (Tib. sem chän) Any being who possesses a mind that is contaminated by delusions or their imprints. Both 'sentient being' and 'living being' are terms used to distinguish beings whose minds are contaminated by either of these two obstructions from Buddhas, whose minds are completely free from these obstructions.

Shariputra One of Buddha Shakyamuni's principal disciples. He has the aspect of a Hinayana Foe Destroyer.

Six realms of samsara See *Samsara*.

Solitary Conqueror A type of Hinayana practitioner. Also known as 'Solitary Realizer'. See also *Hearer*.

Spontaneous bodhichitta Actual bodhichitta. Also known as 'non-fabricated bodhichitta', this mind arises spontaneously day and night. At first we generate an artificial, or fabricated, bodhichitta at certain times by contemplating the suffering of others and so forth, and this acts as the foundation for developing actual bodhichitta.

Supreme Emanation Body See *Emanation Body*.

Ten directions The four cardinal directions, the four intermediate directions, and the directions above and below.

Tenets See *Schools of Buddhist tenets*.

Three realms The three levels within samsara: the desire realm, the form realm, and the formless realm. Beings of the desire realm have powerful delusions, beings of the form realm have more subtle delusions, and beings of the formless realm have very subtle delusions. See also *Desire realm, Form realm,* and *Formless realm.*

Tranquil abiding A concentration that possesses the special bliss of physical and mental suppleness that is attained in dependence upon completing the nine mental abidings. See *Joyful Path of Good Fortune* and *Meaningful to Behold.*

Trijang Rinpoche (AD 1901-1981) A special Tibetan Lama of the twentieth century, who was an emanation of Buddha Shakyamuni, Heruka, Atisha, Amitabha, and Je Tsongkhapa. Also known as 'Trijang Dorjechang' and 'Losang Yeshe'.

Twelve principal deeds The principal deeds of a Supreme Emanation Body: (1) descent from Joyful Land, (2) conception in a mother's womb, (3) birth, (4) mastery of youthful skills and sports, (5) enjoyments with a wife and retinue, (6) ordination, (7) the practice of asceticism, (8) meditation under the Bodhi Tree, (9) overcoming the maras, (10) showing the attainment of enlightenment, (11) turning the Wheel of Dharma, (12) showing the manner of passing away.

Two extremes The extreme of existence (or the extreme of permanence) and the extreme of non-existence (or the extreme of nothingness). With respect to a table that appears to our mind, for example, a non-existent table is an example of an extreme of non-existence and an inherently existent table is an example of an extreme of existence. The table that we see is neither of these two extremes, so neither extreme exists. The table that we see with a valid eye consciousness exists but is empty of inherent existence.

Two obstructions Obstructions to liberation and obstructions to omniscience. Hinayana Foe Destroyers and Bodhisattvas above the seventh ground have abandoned the obstructions to liberation but not the obstructions to omniscience. Consequently, when they are not in meditative equipoise on emptiness objects appear to them as inherently existent.

Vajra Generally the Sanskrit word 'vajra' means indestructible like a diamond and powerful like a thunderbolt. In the context of Secret Mantra it can mean the indivisibility of method and wisdom, omniscient great wisdom, or spontaneous great bliss. It is also the name given to a metal ritual object. See *Tantric Grounds and Paths*.

Vajra posture The perfect cross-legged posture. See *Joyful Path of Good Fortune*.

Vasubandhu A great Indian Buddhist scholar of the fifth century who was converted to the Mahayana by his older brother, Asanga. He wrote *Treasury of Abhidharma* (Skt. *Abhidharmakosha*).

Very subtle mind There are different levels of mind: gross, subtle, and very subtle. Subtle minds manifest when the inner winds gather and dissolve within the central channel. See *Clear Light of Bliss* and *Tantric Grounds and Paths*.

Wheel of Dharma Buddha gave his teachings in three main phases, which are known as 'the three turnings of the Wheel of Dharma'. During the first Wheel he taught the four noble truths, during the second he taught the *Perfection of Wisdom Sutras* and revealed the Madhyamika-Prasangika view, and during the third he taught the Chittamatra view. These teachings were given according to the inclinations and dispositions of his disciples. Buddha's final view is that of the second Wheel.

Wisdom A virtuous, intelligent mind that makes its primary mind realize its object thoroughly. A wisdom is a spiritual path that functions to release our mind from delusions or their imprints. An example of wisdom is the correct view of emptiness. See *Understanding the Mind* and *Ocean of Nectar*.

Yogi/Yogini The Sanskrit word 'Yogi' usually refers to someone who has attained the union of tranquil abiding and superior seeing.

Bibliography

Geshe Kelsang Gyatso is a highly respected meditation master and scholar of the Mahayana Buddhist tradition founded by Je Tsongkhapa. Since arriving in the West in 1977, Geshe Kelsang has worked tirelessly to establish pure Buddhadharma throughout the world. Over this period he has given extensive teachings on the major scriptures of the Mahayana. These teachings are currently being published and provide a comprehensive presentation of the essential Sutra and Tantra practices of Mahayana Buddhism.

Books

The following books by Geshe Kelsang are all published by Tharpa Publications.

The Bodhisattva Vow. The essential practices of Mahayana Buddhism. (2nd. edn., 1995)

Clear Light of Bliss. The practice of Mahamudra in Vajrayana Buddhism. (2nd. edn., 1992)

Eight Steps to Happiness. The Buddhist way of loving kindness. (2000)

Essence of Vajrayana. The Highest Yoga Tantra practice of Heruka body mandala. (1997)

Great Treasury of Merit. The practice of relying upon a Spiritual Guide. (1992)

Guide to Dakini Land. The Highest Yoga Tantra practice of Buddha Vajrayogini. (2nd. edn., 1996)

Heart Jewel. The essential practices of Kadampa Buddhism. (2nd. edn., 1997)

Heart of Wisdom. A commentary to the *Heart Sutra.* (4th. edn., 2001)

Introduction to Buddhism. An explanation of the Buddhist way of life. (2nd. edn., 2001)

Joyful Path of Good Fortune. The complete Buddhist path to enlightenment. (2nd. edn., 1995)

Living Meaningfully, Dying Joyfully. The profound practice of transference of consciousness. (1999)

Meaningful to Behold. The Bodhisattva's way of life. (4th. edn., 1994)

The Meditation Handbook. A practical guide to Buddhist meditation. (3rd. edn., 1995)

Ocean of Nectar. Wisdom and compassion in Mahayana Buddhism. (1995)

Tantric Grounds and Paths. How to enter, progress on, and complete the Vajrayana path. (1994)

Transform Your Life. A blissful journey. (2001)

Understanding the Mind. An explanation of the nature and functions of the mind. (2nd. edn., 1997)

Universal Compassion. Transforming your life through love and compassion. (3rd. edn., 1997)

Sadhanas

Geshe Kelsang has also supervised the translation of a collection
of essential sadhanas, or prayer booklets.

Assembly of Good Fortune. The tsog offering for Heruka body
mandala.

Avalokiteshvara Sadhana. Prayers and requests to the Buddha of
Compassion.

The Bodhisattva's Confession of Moral Downfalls. The purification
practice of the *Mahayana Sutra of the Three Superior Heaps.*

Condensed Essence of Vajrayana. Condensed Heruka body
mandala self-generation sadhana.

Dakini Yoga. Six-session Guru yoga combined with
self-generation as Vajrayogini.

Drop of Essential Nectar. A special fasting and purification
practice in conjunction with Eleven-faced Avalokiteshvara.

Essence of Good Fortune. Prayers for the six preparatory
practices for meditation on the stages of the path to
enlightenment.

Essence of Vajrayana. Heruka body mandala self-generation
sadhana according to the system of Mahasiddha Ghantapa.

Feast of Great Bliss. Vajrayogini self-initiation sadhana.

Great Compassionate Mother. The sadhana of Arya Tara.

Great Liberation of the Mother. Preliminary prayers for
Mahamudra meditation in conjunction with
Vajrayogini practice.

The Great Mother. A method to overcome hindrances and
obstacles by reciting the *Essence of Wisdom Sutra* (the *Heart
Sutra*).

Heartfelt Prayers. Funeral service for cremations and burials.

Heart Jewel. The Guru yoga of Je Tsongkhapa combined with
the condensed sadhana of his Dharma Protector.

The Hundreds of Deities of the Joyful Land. The Guru yoga of
Je Tsongkhapa.

The Kadampa Way of Life. The essential practice of Kadam Lamrim.

Liberation from Sorrow. Praises and requests to the Twenty-one Taras.

Mahayana Refuge Ceremony and Bodhisattva Vow Ceremony.

Medicine Guru Sadhana. The method for making requests to the Assembly of Seven Medicine Buddhas.

Meditation and Recitation of Solitary Vajrasattva.

Melodious Drum Victorious in all Directions. The extensive fulfilling and restoring ritual of the Dharma Protector, the great king Dorje Shugdän, in conjunction with Mahakala, Kalarupa, Kalindewi, and other Dharma Protectors.

Offering to the Spiritual Guide (*Lama Chöpa*). A special Guru yoga practice of Je Tsongkhapa's tradition.

Prayers for Meditation. Brief preparatory prayers for meditation.

A Pure Life. The practice of taking and keeping the eight Mahayana precepts.

The Quick Path. A condensed practice of Heruka Five Deities according to Master Ghantapa's tradition.

Quick Path to Great Bliss. Vajrayogini self-generation sadhana.

Treasury of Blessings. The condensed meaning of Vajrayana Mahamudra and prayers of request to the lineage Gurus.

Treasury of Wisdom. The sadhana of Venerable Manjushri.

Vajra Hero Yoga. A brief essential practice of Heruka body mandala self-generation, and condensed six-session yoga.

Wishfulfilling Jewel. The Guru yoga of Je Tsongkhapa combined with the sadhana of his Dharma Protector.

The Yoga of Buddha Amitayus. A special method for increasing lifespan, wisdom, and merit.

To order any of our publications, or to
receive a catalogue, please contact:

Tharpa Publications
Conishead Priory
Ulverston
Cumbria, LA12 9QQ
England

Tel: 01229-588599
Fax: 01229-483919

E-mail: tharpa@tharpa.com
Website: www.tharpa.com

or

Tharpa Publications
47 Sweeney Road
P.O. Box 430
Glen Spey, NY 12737
USA

Tel: 845-856-5102
Fax: 845-856-2110

Email: tharpa-us@tharpa.com
Website: www.tharpa.com

- NKT -

Study Programmes of Kadampa Buddhism

Kadampa Buddhism is a Mahayana Buddhist school founded by the great Indian Buddhist Master Atisha (AD 982-1054). His followers are known as 'Kadampas'. 'Ka' means 'word' and refers to Buddha's teachings, and 'dam' refers to Atisha's special Lamrim instructions known as 'the stages of the path to enlightenment'. By integrating their knowledge of all Buddha's teachings into their practice of Lamrim, and by integrating this into their everyday lives, Kadampa Buddhists are encouraged to use Buddha's teachings as practical methods for transforming daily activities into the path to enlightenment. The great Kadampa Teachers are famous not only for being great scholars but also for being spiritual practitioners of immense purity and sincerity.

The lineage of these teachings, both their oral transmission and blessings, was then passed from Teacher to disciple, spreading throughout much of Asia, and now to many countries throughout the western world. Buddha's teachings, which are known as 'Dharma', are likened to a wheel that moves from country to country in accordance with changing conditions and people's karmic inclinations. The external forms of presenting Buddhism may change as it meets with different cultures and societies, but

its essential authenticity is ensured through the continuation of
an unbroken lineage of realized practitioners.

Kadampa Buddhism was first introduced into the West in 1977
by the renowned Buddhist Master, Venerable Geshe Kelsang
Gyatso. Since that time he has worked tirelessly to spread
Kadampa Buddhism throughout the world by giving extensive
teachings, writing many profound texts on Kadampa Buddhism,
and founding the New Kadampa Tradition (NKT), which now has
over three hundred and fifty Kadampa Buddhist Centres world-
wide. Each Centre offers study programmes on Buddhist psychol-
ogy, philosophy, and meditation instruction; as well as retreats for
all levels of practitioner. The emphasis is on integrating Buddha's
teachings into daily life to solve our human problems and to
spread lasting peace and happiness throughout the world.

The Kadampa Buddhism of the NKT is an entirely independent
Buddhist tradition and has no political affiliations. It is an associ-
ation of Buddhist Centres and practitioners that derive their
inspiration and guidance from the example of the ancient
Kadampa Buddhist Masters and their teachings, as presented by
Geshe Kelsang Gyatso.

There are three reasons why we need to study and practise the
teachings of Buddha: to develop our wisdom, to cultivate a good
heart, and to maintain a peaceful state of mind. If we do not strive
to develop our wisdom, we shall always remain ignorant of ultimate truth – the true nature of reality. Although we wish for happiness, our ignorance leads us to engage in non-virtuous actions,
which are the main cause of all our suffering. If we do not cultivate a good heart, our selfish motivation destroys harmony and
good relationships with others. We have no peace, and no chance
to gain pure happiness. Without inner peace, outer peace is
impossible. If we do not maintain a peaceful state of mind we are
not happy even if we have ideal conditions. On the other hand,
when our mind is peaceful we are happy even if our external

conditions are unpleasant. Therefore, the development of these qualities is of utmost importance for our daily happiness.

Geshe Kelsang Gyatso, or 'Geshe-la' as he is affectionately called by his students, has designed three special spiritual programmes for the systematic study and practice of Kadampa Buddhism that are especially suited to the modern world – the General Programme (GP), the Foundation Programme (FP), and the Teacher Training Programme (TTP).

GENERAL PROGRAMME

The General Programme provides a basic introduction to Buddhist view, meditation, and practice that is suitable for beginners. It also includes advanced teachings and practices from both Sutra and Tantra.

FOUNDATION PROGRAMME

The Foundation Programme provides an opportunity to deepen our understanding and experience of Buddhism through a systematic study of five texts:

1 *Joyful Path of Good Fortune* – a commentary to Atisha's Lamrim instructions, the stages of the path to enlightenment.
2 *Universal Compassion* – a commentary to Bodhisattva Chekhawa's *Training the Mind in Seven Points*.
3 *Heart of Wisdom* – a commentary to the *Heart Sutra*.
4 *Meaningful to Behold* – a commentary to Venerable Shantideva's *Guide to the Bodhisattva's Way of Life*.
5 *Understanding the Mind* – a detailed explanation of the mind based on the works of the Buddhist scholars Dharmakirti and Dignaga.

The benefits of studying and practising these texts are as follows:

(1) *Joyful Path of Good Fortune* – we gain the ability to put all Buddha's teachings of both Sutra and Tantra into practice. We can easily make progress on and complete the stages of the path to the supreme happiness of enlightenment. From a practical point of view, Lamrim is the main body of Buddha's teachings, and the other teachings are like its limbs.

(2) *Universal Compassion* – we gain the ability to integrate Buddha's teachings into our daily lives and solve all our human problems.

(3) *Heart of Wisdom* – we gain a realization of the ultimate nature of reality. By gaining this realization we can eliminate the ignorance of self-grasping, which is the root of all our suffering.

(4) *Meaningful to Behold* – we transform our daily activities into the Bodhisattva's way of life, thereby making every moment of our human life meaningful.

(5) *Understanding the Mind* – we understand the relationship between our mind and its external objects. If we understand that objects depend upon the subjective mind, we can change the way objects appear to us by changing our own mind. Gradually we shall gain the ability to control our mind and in this way solve all our problems.

TEACHER TRAINING PROGRAMME

The Teacher Training Programme is designed for people who wish to train as authentic Dharma Teachers. In addition to completing the study of twelve texts of Sutra and Tantra, which include the five texts mentioned above, the student is required to observe certain commitments with regard to behaviour and way of life, and to complete a number of meditation retreats.

All Kadampa Buddhist Centres are open to the public. Every year we celebrate Festivals in the USA and Europe, including two in England, where people gather from around the world to receive special teachings and empowerments and to enjoy a spiritual holiday. Please feel free to visit us at any time!

For further information, please contact:

UK NKT Office
Conishead Priory
Ulverston
Cumbria, LA12 9QQ
England

Tel/Fax: 01229-588533

Email: kadampa@dircon.co.uk
Website: www.kadampa.org

or

US NKT Office
Kadampa Meditation Center
47 Sweeney Road
P.O. Box 447
Glen Spey, NY 12737
USA

Tel: 845-856-9000
Fax: 845-856-2110

Email: KadampaCenter@aol.com
Website: www.kadampacenter.org

Index

The letter 'g' indicates an entry in the glossary.